THE BIBLE: THE COMPLETE WORD OF GOD (*abridged*)

Adam Long, Reed Martin & Austin Tichenor

Additional Material by Matthew Croke

BROADWAY PLAY PUBLISHING INC
56 E 81st St., NY NY 10028-0202
212 772-8334 fax: 212 772-8358
http://www.BroadwayPlayPubl.com

Music, which is available to licensees from Broadway
Play Publishing Inc, was transcribed by Jon Weber.
That's Armageddon music composed by Jon Weber.

First printing: December 2000
I S B N: 0-88145-182-7

Book design: Marie Donovan
Word processing: Microsoft Word for Windows
Typographic controls: Xerox Ventura Publisher 2.0 P E
Typeface: Palatino
Copy editing: Michele Travis
Printed on recycled acid-free paper and bound in the
U S A

IMPORTANT NOTE

The name "REDUCED SHAKESPEARE COMPANY®" is a Registered Trademark, and its use in any way whatsoever to publicize, promote or advertise any performance of this script IS EXPRESSLY PROHIBITED.

Likewise, any use of the name "REDUCED SHAKESPEARE COMPANY®" within the actual live performance of this script IS ALSO EXPRESSLY PROHIBITED.

The play must be billed as follows:

THE BIBLE: THE COMPLETE WORD OF GOD
(abridged)
by
Adam Long, Reed Martin & Austin Tichenor

Additional Material by Matthew Croke

ABOUT THE AUTHORS

Adam Long. Adam lives in a little house in North London with his wife Alex, his son Joe, their friend John, and a stray cat who regularly attacks every member of the family. Adam is the proud holder of a British driver's license. He cites his influences as Harpo Marx, Dogen Zenji, and the Grateful Dead.

Reed Martin has co-authored two other plays with The Reduced Shakespeare Company—THE COMPLETE HISTORY OF AMERICA (abridged) and THE COMPLETE MILLENNIUM MUSICAL (abridged) and contributed additional material to THE COMPLETE WORKS OF WILLIAM SHAKESPEARE (abridged). He has written for the B B C, National Public Radio, Britain's Channel Four, R T E Ireland, Public Radio International, the Washington Post, and Vogue magazine. Prior to joining the Reduced Shakespeare Company, Reed was a Clown and Assistant Ringmaster with Ringling Brothers/Barnum & Bailey Circus. He has a B A in Political Science/ Theater from U C Berkeley and an M F A in Acting from U C San Diego. He is a member of the Dramatists Guild. He lives in Northern California with his wife and sons.

Austin Tichenor. For the Reduced Shakespeare Company, Austin is the co-author of the stage plays THE COMPLETE HISTORY OF AMERICA (abridged) and THE COMPLETE MILLENNIUM MUSICAL (abridged), the half-hour T V film *The Ring Reduced*, and the radio productions of *The Reduced Shakespeare Radio Show* (B B C), *The Reduced Shakespeare Company Round Table* (N P R's *All Things Considered*), and *The Reduced Shakespeare Company Christmas* (Public Radio International). He also is author of over twenty plays and musicals for young audiences, and with Reed Martin is the co-author of the book *The Greatest Story Ever Sold* available from Westminster/John Knox Press. He is a member of the Dramatists Guild and lives in Los Angeles where he is hard at work on three screenplays, a novel, and his wife.

The Writers would like to thank Alex Jackson-Long, Jane Martin, Dee Ryan, Rick Reiser, Steve Smith, Reverend Alan Piotter, Reverend James Knutson, Deborah Bornstein Sosebee, Stephen Gray, Susan Leigh, Cathy Davis, Bill Matson, Robert Seigel, Philip Proctor, University of Alaska at Anchorage, Pier One Theater of Homer Alaska, American Repertory Theater, Reston (Virginia) Community Center, The Kennedy Center, and the Tichenor Ranch.

THE BIBLE: THE COMPLETE WORD OF GOD
(abridged) was originally produced and performed
by The Reduced Shakespeare Company. It had its first
public performance on 24 March 1995 at the University
of Alaska at Anchorage. In March and April 1995 the
play was presented at the Pier One Theater of Homer,
Alaska and at the American Repertory Theater of
Cambridge, Massachusetts. Later that summer it ran for
seven weeks at the Kennedy Center in Washington, DC.
With one cast change, the play had a limited eight-week
engagement at the Gielgud Theatre in London's West
End beginning 8 August 1997.

ORIGINAL CAST

Matthew Croke
Reed Martin
Austin Tichenor

WEST END CAST

Reed Martin
Matt Rippy
Austin Tichenor

FOR WHAT IT'S WORTH

Although we use the names Matt, Reed, and Austin within the script, each cast member should use his own real name when performing the show.

There are a number of topical references in the script. The humor and relevance of these will fade over time, so we encourage each production to change these references to keep them as up-to-date as possible.

The production elements described in the script are from the original production by the Reduced Shakespeare Company. Consequently, the scenery, props, and costumes were all "reduced" in both quality and number. You will not be so encumbered, and may be tempted to use real explosions, live animals, and leggy showgirls. This sounds like fun, but may falsely raise audience expectations.

It has been our experience that the script works best when performed seriously. That is to say, if the script is funny, play it straight. Basically we adhered to two rules:
Rule #1: Less Is More; and
Rule #2: Camp Is Bad...except for possibly at the end during *That's Armageddon* and even then a little bit goes a long way (see Rule #1).

This script is an authentic re-creation of Biblical stories and anecdotes so the jokes are as old as Moses' toes and twice as corny. For God's sake, don't linger. Drop your load and keep moving. Don't let the audience get ahead of you, because when they do it isn't pretty.

ACT ONE

(Dramatic music Thus Spake Zarathustra *begins. The houselights go out. All is dark.)*

V O: In the beginning, there was...chaos.

(At the appropriate musical peak, a spotlight comes up on AUSTIN—*naked, with a fig leaf over his groin. Blackout)*

(At the next musical crash, the spotlight comes up again on AUSTIN *standing next to* MATT, *who is also naked and wears a woman's blond wig, with three fig leaves, over each breast and his groin. Blackout)*

(And finally, on the final musical crash, the spotlight reveals the first two joined by REED *standing between them.* REED *is also naked, with one teeny-weeny fig leaf over his groin.)*

*(*AUSTIN *and* MATT *look at what* REED's *wearing and shake their heads. Blackout)*

V O: And lo the actors did put their clothes on. And the audience was well-pleased.

(The lights come up again on Our Three Heroes. They're each wearing Biblical robes, sandals, and black sunglasses. AUSTIN *stands at a keyboard down left,* REED *wears his accordion,* MATT *holds a tambourine.)*

(With a strong downbeat, REED *plays the accordion,* AUSTIN *snaps his fingers, and* MATT *beats with his tambourine. They sing.)*

AUSTIN: In the beginning
Everything was void
God saw all that emptiness
He really got annoyed
So He started His creatin'
Because He knew He should
He said:

REED: "Let there be light!"

(Full lights up on stage)

REED: "Wow, that light is good!"

(Lights crossfade back to just the three specials. The guys start dancing a very simple dance which mostly involves stepping to the left and then to the right.)

AUSTIN: Then He got down to dividing
On day one and day two and day three
He divided the dark from the light
He divided the earth from the sea

MATT: He divided the water and firmament
Divided the day and the night

REED: But then He let out a heavy sigh
'Cause it still didn't feel quite right

AUSTIN: From the top of His hallowed head
To the soles of His holy shoes

ALL: He had a serious case
Of the "In the beginning blues"

REED: On Wednesday He made vegetables

MATT: On Thursday celestial light

REED: On Friday He made poultry and fish

AUSTIN: On Saturday He partied all night
Making cattle and oxen and turtles and lizards and

rabbits and gophers and hamsters and sheep and
some stoats—It's a kind of weasel.

REED: In His own image He made man

AUSTIN: And God said:

*(Music stops and all three start snapping in rhythm. AUSTIN
speaks in rhythm, gesturing dramatically. When he gestures,
MATT strikes his tambourine and REED plays a chord for
emphasis.)*

AUSTIN: Be fruitful and multiply, and replenish the
earth and subdue it.
    And have dominion over the fish of the sea and the
fowl of the air and every living thing that moves.
    And the Lord said, BEHOLD! I give unto thee the
power to reason and think and imagine!
    And the Lord said, BEHOLD! I give unto thee
commerce, imperialism, industrial revolution!
    And the Lord said, BEHOLD! I give unto thee
morphine and penicillin and marijuana. You got the
right one, Baby!
    And the Lord said, BEHOLD! I give unto thee
suburbia *(Point)*, and shopping malls *(Point)*, and
overpopulation, ozone depletion and Perry Mason!
(Point) (Point) (Point)
    And do you realize that in the next ten years every
single species in the world will have its own Web site?
(Point)
    And then the Lord *(Point)* and then the Lord said
(Point) (Point) the Lord said *(Point) (Point) (Point)*
...I forgot where I was...

REED/MATT: Seventh day.

AUSTIN: Right! *(Singing)*
On the seventh day God rested
Cuz He had nothing to lose

ALL: He had a serious case of the
In the beginning blues.

AUSTIN: Why was the Almighty so blue?

REED: Why wasn't He having a ball?

ALL: If He knew how depressing the world would turn out
He would never have started at all!

AUSTIN: Take it Matthew!

(MATT *whips out a harmonica and microphone and kicks out an amazing solo that rips through the entire next verse.*)

ALL: He had a serious case of those earth without form
Void and nothingness
Darkness and emptiness
In the beginning blues

(*Big finish. Blackout.* MATT *and* REED *ditch their instruments. Lights up*)

AUSTIN: Good evening, ladies and gentlemen.
I'm Austin Tichenor—

REED: I'm Reed Martin—

MATT: I'm Matt Croke—

AUSTIN: ...and welcome to the _____ Theater and tonight's performance of THE BIBLE: THE COMPLETE WORD OF GOD (abridged).

REED: Tonight we'll be taking you on a marvelous, spiritual journey.

MATT: A marvelous, spiritual journey.

AUSTIN: Call it a mission.

MATT: A mission!

REED: A quest, if you will.

MATT: A quest, if you will!

AUSTIN: Matt, go get the books.

MATT: Matt, go get the... *(He realizes he's been had. Under his breath:)* This sucks. *(He exits.)*

AUSTIN: Call it a journey towards enlightenment and inner peace as we present to you, in its entirety, The Bible—the Greatest Story Ever Accepted as Fact.

(MATT reenters with three books. He hands one each to AUSTIN and REED.)

MATT: And tonight we'll explain it all. We will shine a bright light on its mysteries.

REED: Make the unknown known.

AUSTIN: The inexplicable plicable.

REED: And I think it's important to point out that although this show is about the Bible, it is not about any particular religion which uses the Bible as a sacred text.

AUSTIN: That's right. It is certainly not our intention to slander or in any way impugn Christians, or Jews, or Muslims....

MATT: Or Buddhists or Hindus or Transcendentalists...

REED: Or Zoroastrians or Druids or agnostics...

AUSTIN: Or Catholics or any cult members of any kind. It's not what we want to do....

REED: No, why would you?

MATT: And I think we should start the show out by sharing the research materials we used.

REED: Good idea. *(Takes a book and holds it up)* Well, I went straight to the source: the King James Edition of the Holy Bible. Now, we intend to cover the Old Testament in the first act, New Testament in the second act, and just for our own information up here—by applause—how many of you here tonight have read any portion of The Bible?

(Audience applauds. AUSTIN *points.)*

AUSTIN: There's a couple of pagans right there who haven't.

REED: Well, they've come to the right place. And just to take it a step further, and this time just by a show of hands, has anyone here tonight read The Bible cover to cover? *(A few hands are raised.)* It looks like we've got our work cut out for us. That's okay, though, because in preparing for this show I have done extensive research on the Bible.

AUSTIN: Reed, as a result of your extensive research, do you now believe the Bible should be taken literally?

REED: Yes, Austin, I do.

AUSTIN: Really?

REED: Yes. In fact, I literally took this Bible from my hotel room.

AUSTIN: Okay. *(Takes a book and holds it up)* I relied heavily on *Isaac Asimov's Guide to the Bible* for a greater understanding of the Good Book's geographical and historical context, as well as an appreciation of the pagan myths and ancient Hebrew texts that underlie the Bible's classic stories.

MATT: *(Holds up his book)* I used the *Children's Illustrated Bible*. It's great, it has everything in it: Adam and Eve, David and Goliath, Cain and Abel...

AUSTIN: Sodom and Gomorra...

MATT: Who?

AUSTIN: Sodom and Gomorra.

MATT: Um, no, it didn't have them.

REED: Abraham sacrificing his son Isaac.

MATT: Get out. That happened?

REED: It almost did.

MATT: Really?

AUSTIN: Yeah, isn't that in there?

MATT: No. It just has the happy stories.

AUSTIN: You mean, like Cain and Abel? That was a real happy story.

MATT: It was, Austin! Apparently you didn't read it. Like when Cain takes Abel out to the fields, where Abel thinks he's going to be killed, and Cain raises up in his hand two tickets to the land of milk and honey, where they get to ride the ponies and get sick on cotton candy but when they get home their mother isn't angry and kisses them goodnight.

(REED and AUSTIN look at each other.)

REED/AUSTIN: What?

MATT: Didn't you read it?

REED	AUSTIN:
No.	Not that part.

MATT: Well, did you read about how when Moses and Jesus were babies, and their parents thought they were going to be killed. And then Pharaoh and Herod took all the boy babies out to the land of milk and honey, where they got to ride the ponies and got sick on cotton candy but when they got home, their mother wasn't angry and kisses them goodnight?

AUSTIN: Matt, is that the only research book you read to prepare for this?

MATT: No! I also read *Women on Top* by Nancy Friday. *(He reaches into his waistband and pulls out a copy.)*

REED/AUSTIN: Oh, that's good, that's better....

REED: Well, Matt, did you read anything about Noah's Ark, because as you know, it's my favorite Bible story?

MATT: And rightly so, Reed. It's all about how Noah gathered up all the animals onto the ark...

REED/AUSTIN: Yeah...

MATT: And then it started to rain...

REED/AUSTIN: Yeah...

MATT: And all the wicked people swam off to the land of milk and honey...

REED/AUSTIN: No...

MATT: Yes, and then they discover that the talking ponies are just a phallic extension of a woman's desire for sexual domination, and when they get home their mother says Freud was right...!

(REED exits in disgust with MATT in hot pursuit.)

AUSTIN: Well, it looks like Matt's medication just kicked in, so we should get going.

(The lights fade to black except for the spot on AUSTIN.)

AUSTIN: Ladies and gentlemen, our first reading tonight is from the early part of Genesis, which many scholars argue is the definitive part of Genesis, because that's when they still had Peter Gabriel. *(If there's applause, he says, "I see some scholars here tonight agree.")* Let us begin. *(Reading)* "And the Lord God caused a deep sleep to fall upon Adam, and he slept: and God took one of Adam's ribs and made he a woman, and brought her unto the man."

(Spotlight up on REED *lying down right.* AUSTIN *plays spooky music as* REED *begins to writhe like John Hurt in Alien. Finally, "Eve" bursts out of* REED's *stomach [really, it's a hand-puppet of Eve with three fig leaves, operated by* REED. *This is accomplished by* REED *wearing a tunic with one sleeve stuffed, with a fake hand at the end]).*

REED/EVE: Good morning! Let the downfall of Man begin! Nyah-ha-ha!!

(Blackout. Light up on AUSTIN*)*

AUSTIN: *(Still "reading" from the Bible)* And the Lord God looked down on Adam and Eve bickering and knew they had eaten of the forbidden fruit. And he waxed Wroth, which gave Wroth a lustrous sheen. And the Lord cursed the wicked serpent and said that from that day forth the serpent would slither on its belly. Presumably, the serpent had legs prior to that, indicating that it was more likely a wicked lizard. And the Lord God bethought himself that Wicked Lizard would be a good name for a band. *(He exits.)*

(Lights up on REED *and* MATT.*)*

MATT: And so it was that the Lord God sent Adam and Eve forth from the Garden of Eden.

REED: And Adam knew Eve his wife, in fact, he knew her extremely well for there was no one else to hang out with; and she conceived, and bore Cain.

MATT: And she conceived again, and bore his brother Abel.

AUSTIN: *(Offstage, over God mic)* Hello, Cain.

REED: Hello, God.

AUSTIN: Hello Abel.

MATT: Hello God.

AUSTIN: Do you boys have offerings for me today?

BOTH: Yes.

AUSTIN: Good! Let's take a look.

MATT: I have brought you the firstlings of my flock and the fat thereof. (*He holds up a giant can of Spam.*)

AUSTIN: Thank you, Abel!

REED: I have brought the Fruit of the Loom as an offering unto thee. (*He holds up a tie or a pair of underwear.*)

AUSTIN: Cain, that is the same thing you get me every year. Now you two go off and play in the field. Oh, and Cain—

REED: Yes, God?

AUSTIN: Remember—you are your brother's keeper.

REED: Oh, I'll keep him alright. Hey Abel, come here! Look—it's the land of milk and honey!

MATT: Oh boy!

(MATT *exits behind the center drop. Still in the view of the audience,* REED *takes* MATT's *club, and swings the club savagely, brushing the center drop. Cymbal crash. The illusion is that* REED *has clubbed* MATT.)

MATT: (*Offstage scream*) Ow!

(AUSTIN *enters.*)

AUSTIN: And God placed a mark upon Cain.

(MATT *enters and hangs a sign on* REED *that reads "Mark" and then points to the wings.* REED *exits followed by* MATT.)

AUSTIN: Now, this brings us up to Chapter Five of Genesis, which is the genealogy of Adam. Now this is a pretty complicated section, so I've asked Matt to—Matt, would you bring out that chart?

MATT: (*Off*) Yeah!

AUSTIN: This chart will help diagram the many generations that are descended from Adam, and you'll all get a very clear....

(AUSTIN *holds out his left arm in presentation mode, as if* MATT *is rolling on something huge. Instead,* MATT *hands him a single white sheet of paper, on which ADAM and his descendants are computer-printed.*)

AUSTIN: What is this?

MATT: That chart. You told me to photocopy it.

AUSTIN: You were supposed to enlarge it. It's supposed to be a visual aid for...they can't see...(*To audience*) can you see this? Never mind, Matt, forget it, I'll deal with it.

(MATT *exits.*)

AUSTIN: Look, I apologize for this. I'll just read this out loud to you. It won't be quite the the same as actually seeing it up close, but I think you'll still get a very clear sense...

(MATT *re-enters and heaves a stack of photocopied charts [maybe fifty] out into the audience. They cascade everywhere.* AUSTIN *waits for everything to settle, then plows on as if this weren't scripted and actually published right here on page 11 of the script.*)

AUSTIN: So if you can just pass those around...make sure you get some up to the people in the back in the cheap seats. Oh, you two are sharing? Very Christian of you. Now please, read along silently while I read the chart aloud. The Generations of Adam. (*He recites and makes his way to the keyboard.*)
Now Adam begat Cain who begat Enoch and then Irad
(*Pronounced, "eye-red"*)
Mehujael, Methusael, and still he wasn't tired
(*Pronounced, "tie-red"*)
Then Lamech who begat Jabal and Jubal who were

brothers
And Tubalcain and Naamah and many many others!

(AUSTIN *strikes a chord and sings. The light goes to a special on the keyboard.*)

AUSTIN: Begattin', begattin'
Everywhere begattin'
Begattin' like the bunnies like to do
They were begattin', begattin'
Makin' babies happen
'Cause back then there was nothing else to do!

And Adam begat Seth who begat Enos then Cainan
Mahalaleel and Jared with no energy declinin'
Jared begat Enoch because there was nothing to it
Methusaleh is proof you never get too old to do it

Begattin', begattin'
Everywhere begattin'
Methuselah would surely leave his mark
He was begattin', begattin'
Makin' babies happen
He begat Noah who then begat the ark

(REED *and* MATT *step in behind* AUSTIN *and begin to harmonise—singing "Ooohs" and "Aaahs".*)

AUSTIN: They were begattin' in the fields
Begattin' in the straw
Begattin' fully clothed
Begattin' in the raw

They were begattin' on the sea
Begattin' on the land
Begattin' with a partner
Is better than your hand

So go...

ALL: ...Begattin', begattin'
Everywhere begattin'
'Cause back then there was nothing else to do!

(Blackout. A spot comes up down right, which reveals REED *holding a beautiful hand-carved Ark which is filled with little, carved pairs of animals.)*

REED: The Ark. Noah's Ark, the most famous ark in the entire history of arks! What I have here in my hands is an exact replica, as far as can be scientifically determined, of Noah's Ark that I have personally carved over the last nine years out of genuine gopherwood I imported from the Middle East.

*(*MATT *and* AUSTIN *enter and applaud under the last few words of* REED's *speech. They are a bit patronizing.)*

MATT/AUSTIN: Wow! Good job!

REED: Thank you. Now you see Noah there? Noah alone took me seven months because I used genuine stone-age carving tools.

*(*AUSTIN *points to two of the animals.)*

AUSTIN: Hey, look at those two...

REED: Yeah, those two are begattin'.

MATT: So—let's move on....

*(*MATT *and* AUSTIN *start to exit.)*

REED: What about Noah's Ark?

AUSTIN: We just did it.

REED: No, we didn't DO Noah's Ark. We introduced Noah's Ark. But we didn't DO Noah's Ark.

(They start to exit again.)

AUSTIN: That's all we need to do.

REED: No, there's a lot of unanswered questions about Noah Ark.

AUSTIN: Like what?

REED: Were there dinosaurs on the Ark?

AUSTIN: Yes.

REED: They're not mentioned in the Bible.

AUSTIN: So what? There's a lot of things not mentioned in the Bible. Handguns aren't mentioned in the Bible, telephones aren't mentioned, computers aren't mentioned—

MATT: Wait a minute! Computers were on Noah's Ark?

AUSTIN: No. Don't be silly. Computers were in the Garden of Eden.

REED: Matt, we covered this. Eve had an Apple.

AUSTIN: Right? Eve had an Apple and Adam had a Wang.

REED: Remember this? We discussed this.

MATT: Right...

(MATT *and* AUSTIN *start to exit, but see* REED *continuing.* MATT *crosses down to him.*)

REED: *(To audience)* Now if you look very closely at the male piglet there, I think you can see the painstaking detail...

MATT: Stop it, Reed, you're boring everybody.

REED: No, I'm not.

MATT: Yes, you are. Listen to me: the story of Noah's Ark is so overdone, everybody knows it, and besides, it probably never happened.

(Sound cue: a startling "horror movie" type chord as REED's *face registers shock. The lights snap to a special on* REED. MATT *and* AUSTIN *freeze.)*

REED: Never happened!?! Never happened!?! Why, they might as well say that the whole Bible never happened! What do they think is up there on Mount Ararat, anyway—The Titanic? They might as well strip me of my childlike faith and innocence. They might as well mock Matt because he's never kissed a girl! They might as well tell all of you that I still occasionally wet the bed!!!! Aaaaaaaa!!!!!!!!

(As REED *screams, the lights shift back to a day state.* AUSTIN *and* MATT *unfreeze.)*

AUSTIN: Reed, you still wet the bed?

MATT: Eeeuwww.

REED: Look, stop listening to my inner monologue! Now, where are we?

AUSTIN: We just did Noah's Ark.

REED: We did?

AUSTIN/MATT: Yeah.

REED: Well, if we just did Noah's Ark, then we're still in Genesis—Chapter Ten. And after that there's thirty-eight more books in the Old Testament alone!

AUSTIN: Thirty-eight more books?! We better haul ass.

ALL: Tower of Babel!

*(*MATT *and* AUSTIN *exit. Lights go to a special on* REED.)*

REED: And the whole earth was of one tribe and one language. And the people said to one another, "Go to," which is Biblical for "Up Yours." "Go to, let us build a tower whose top may reach unto heaven."

(REED *exits. Lights comes up on* MATT *dressed as a woman making out furiously with* AUSTIN. *One of them holds a sign which says "BEFORE TOWER".*)

MATT/CAP: Oh Shem!

AUSTIN/SHEM: Oh Caphtorim!

(*Enter* REED *as* NIMROD. *He carries a briefcase, which he sets down.*)

REED/NIM: Honey! I'm home.

MATT/CAP: Nimrod!

REED/NIM: Shem?! Caphtorim?! What's going on?!

MATT/CAP: We can't hide it any longer! Shem and I know each other.

REED/NIM: Oh NOW I get it! Everyday, while I've been off building a tower, you two behind my back, have been entwining yourselves in sordid, unnatural, immoral...um....

AUSTIN/SHEM: Disgusting.

REED/NIM: Thank you...disgusting knowledge!

MATT/CAP: There's more to life than tower building, Nimrod. But you wouldn't understand that!

REED/NIM: But don't you see? I'm doing it for you, and for our children, and for our children's children.

AUSTIN/SHEM: Has it not occurred to you that God will punish us for trying to be His equal?

REED/NIM: Impossible! We're of one tribe and one language and we can do anything! *That* is why we're building a tower to God!

MATT/CAP: Oh, please! You're building that tower because you have a teeny weenie.

REED/NIM: Go to! I thought I knew you, Caphtorim.

(MATT *pounds on* REED's *chest while* REED *says in a low tone, "Aaahhh."*)

MATT/CAP: You never really knew me. But Shem knows me two, three, even four times a night.

REED/NIM: Shem! How could you!?!

AUSTIN/SHEM: Raw oysters and ginseng!

MATT/CAP: Come on, Shem, let's get out of here.

(MATT *and* AUSTIN *start to exit.* REED *pulls a picture of a bomb from his briefcase.*)

REED/NIM: Hold it right there! You two aren't going anywhere.

AUSTIN/SHEM: Lookout! He's got a picture of a bomb!

(REED *laughs maniacally.* MATT *and* AUSTIN *scream.* REED *flips the picture to reveal another picture of a blast and the word "BOOM". Blackout. Lights up. The scene begins again, identically, except that as* MATT *and* AUSTIN *are making out, one of them holds a sign which reads "AFTER TOWER".*)

MATT/CAP: Oh Shem!

AUSTIN/SHEM: Konichiwa, Miyoshi! Hai!

(*Enter* REED *as* NIMROD. *He carries a briefcase, which he sets down.*)

REED/NIM: Mi amor, aquí estoy!

MATT/CAP: Nimrod!

REED/NIM: José!?! Maria!?! Qué pasó aquí?

MATT/CAP: We can't hide it any longer, Nimrod! Shem and I know each other.

REED/NIM: Sacro bambino! Mi diggie diggie buildy molto dios! Y ustedes bahdha bing bahdha boom dans la bouncie bouncie!?! Ustedes son sordido, stencho, grossamente...um...

AUSTIN/SHEM: Disgustivo des ka?

REED/NIM: Gracias...disgustivo yo quiero Taco Bell.

MATT/CAP: There's more to life than tower building, Nimrod. But you wouldn't understand that!

REED/NIM: No comprendes? Lo he hecho para tí, y para nuestros hijos, y para los hijos de nuestros hijos!

AUSTIN/SHEM: Bacca geijing! Buddha shinto mushy-mushy, Godzilla killy-killy sukiyaki?!

REED/NIM: Besa mí culo! Taco sombrero Antonio Banderas!

MATT/CAP: Oh, please. You're building that tower because you have a teeny weenie.

REED/NIM: Poquito chequito?

(MATT *pounds on* REED's *chest while* REED *says in a high tone,* "Ehhhhhhh.")

MATT/CAP: You never really knew me. But Shem knows me two, three, even four times a night.

REED/NIM: Comó pudistes, José?

AUSTIN/SHEM: Saké and sushi! Hai!

MATT/CAP: Come on, Shem, let's get out of here.

(MATT *and* AUSTIN *start to exit.* REED *pulls a picture of a bomb from his briefcase.*)

REED/NIM: Alto! No mueven!

AUSTIN/SHEM: Ohhh! Tora, tora, tora!

(REED *laughs maniacally.* MATT *and* AUSTIN *scream.* REED *drops the picture to reveal another picture of a blast*

and the words "EL BOOMO!" Blackout. Lights up on
MATT)

MATT: So then the Lord dispersed the people—those
who spoke Japanese to Japan, those who spoke Cuban
to Florida, and those who spoke Babel to Washington,
D C. Which brings us now, of course, to Abraham.

(Battle Hymn of the Republic *plays.* REED *enters wearing
a black stove-pipe hat and black beard.*)

REED/ABRAHAM: Thank you, Lord, for delivering me
into the Land of Canaan four score and seventeen
seconds ago.

AUSTIN/GOD: *(On mic)* You're welcome, Abraham.
Are you happy to be down there in Canaan?

REED/ABRAHAM: Yes, Lord!

AUSTIN/GOD: *(On mic)* What would you give me to
ensure that you and your descendants live in Canaan
forever?

REED/ABRAHAM: Oh, I would give anything, my Lord!

AUSTIN/GOD: *(On mic)* Good. Give me the foreskin
from your penis.

(Pause)

REED/ABRAHAM: Excuse me?

AUSTIN/GOD: *(On mic)* Give me the foreskin from your
penis.

REED/ABRAHAM: That's what I thought you said. But
I'm confused. What's a foreskin?

AUSTIN/GOD: *(On mic)* The foreskin is that useless piece
of flesh at the end of the penis.

REED/ABRAHAM: I thought that was a man.

AUSTIN/GOD: *(On mic)* No, I meant the other end.

REED/ABRAHAM: Ohh.

AUSTIN/GOD: *(On mic)* This will be a covenant between me and thee, Abraham. You will be a knight in my army. I will dub thee Sir Cumcision.

REED/ABRAHAM: But why? Why do you want my foreskin?

AUSTIN/GOD: *(On mic)* I'm making a wallet. When I rub it, it'll turn into a suitcase. Ha-ha-ha! But seriously, Abraham. In the future, you can circumcise your male children when they are babies and it won't hurt as much.

REED/ABRAHAM: I'm glad you're so concerned about my children.

AUSTIN/GOD: *(On mic)* Speaking of your children, I'd like to speak to you about Isaac.

REED/ABRAHAM: What about him?

AUSTIN/GOD: *(On mic)* I'd like you to kill him.

(Pause)

REED/ABRAHAM: Excuse me?

AUSTIN/GOD: *(On mic)* I'd like you to ki—

REED/ABRAHAM: I heard you!

AUSTIN/GOD: *(On mic)* Place him upon a burnt offering and sacrifice his life to me.

REED/ABRAHAM: Isn't this all a little pagan for a supposedly monotheistic religion?

AUSTIN/GOD: *(On mic)* Pagan, shmagan. Do you live in fear of me or not?

REED/ABRAHAM: Yes, Lord! I will sacrifice Isaac to you!

AUSTIN/GOD: *(On mic)* Really?

REED/ABRAHAM: Yes, this very day! Sara, bring me the boy!

(MATT *runs on carrying a baby and a big knife. Without stopping, he hands both to* REED *and exits.*)

REED/ABRAHAM: Here, Lord! Here is my son Isaac, for whom my wife Sara and I waited for many years! (REED *looks at the doll.*) He's a little small for an eleven-year old. I pledge his life to you! (*He raises up the knife.*)

AUSTIN/GOD: (*On mic*) What are you doing?!

REED/ABRAHAM: I'm killing my son for you, Lord!

AUSTIN/GOD: (*On mic*) I was kidding! Why do all you fundamentalists have no sense of humor?

(REED *shrugs. Blackout. Lights up.* AUSTIN *runs on.*)

AUSTIN: Isaac survived the circumcision and grew up and had two strapping sons—Esau and Jacob. Esau was the oldest—

(MATT *enters wearing a black wig backwards to cover his face and another wig hanging out from the waist of his trousers.*)

AUSTIN: —and had long hair all over his body.

(REED *enters.*)

AUSTIN: Jacob, on the other hand...didn't.

(MATT *and* REED *exit.*)

AUSTIN: Jacob swindled Esau out of his inheritance, and when Esau discovered this, he wanted to kill him. But Jacob escaped swiftly to the land of Haran, where he saw two sisters tending a flock of sheep.

(MATT *enters, looking delectable wearing a wig and skirt.*)

AUSTIN: The first was Rachel, who was extraordinarily beautiful.

(REED *enters, dressed horrifically—eyes crossed, fright wig, ugly false teeth.*)

AUSTIN: The second was Leah, who was...you know what, she had a great personality. And a wonderful sense of humor and she was really fertile....

REED: All right, stop it. Just stop it.

AUSTIN: What?

REED: Just stop it. The point is that Jacob loved Rachel because she was the prettiest, blah blah blah. Well, it's always the prettiest, isn't it? And through tricks and deception he ends up marrying Leah instead, and even though the ugly one bears him many fine sons he still loves the pretty one so he marries her, too, which you could do in Bible times. And then, in a great twist of Biblical irony—something the Bible is not particularly known for, by the way—it turns out that Rachel—the pretty one, the one Jacob loves so much—is completely barren—can't have any kids! So what happens? God takes pity on poor, poor Rachel. Why? Oh, I don't know—could it be because she's babe-alicious?! And everybody's always doing Rachel favors because she's so foxy?! I don't know—read into it what you will. So God allows her to conceive and bear a child and, surprise, surprise, surprise, the kid turns out to be Jacob's favorite—he names him Joseph. I mean, the whole moral of the story is that God loves beautiful people more than he loves ugly people!!

(*Pause*)

AUSTIN: Reed, this is really more about you than it is about Jacob, isn't it?

(REED *shrugs.*)

AUSTIN: Let's just move on....

REED: Yes. Jacob, Father of Joseph. (*He exits.*)

AUSTIN: Right. Joseph was the owner—

MATT: Hey, Austin, can I do this? I've been doing some research.

AUSTIN: Oh, okay, sure. *(He starts to go.)*

MATT: Joseph, the father of Jesus! He was—

AUSTIN: NO!! Wait, Matt, you're confused. You're thinking of a different Joseph, a later, latter-day Joseph.

MATT: Wait—Jesus' father was a Mormon?

AUSTIN: No. Of course not. Jesus' father was a Jew.

MATT: Jesus' father was a Jew? Wait a second. You mean Jesus Christ was a Jew?

(REED enters.)

AUSTIN: Well, he was Jew-ish, y'know? He was kind of a Jew...

REED: Yeah, the Joseph I'm talking about is from the amazing technicolor musical.

MATT: Oh, by Andrew Lloyd Webber! Wait a minute, I know something about Andrew Lloyd Webber, what is it? Oh yeah, I hate Andrew Lloyd Webber!

AUSTIN: Me, too!

REED: Me three!

MATT: Shall we move on?

AUSTIN/REED: Yes!

REED: Genesis, Exodus!

MATT: All right. I'll do this, Reed, I screwed up the last one.

REED: *(As he's exiting)* Okay!

MATT: We now move on to the book of Exodus, where we join Moses talking to the burning bush, already in progress.

(REED *enters with the Burning Bush—three burning torches. He kneels downstage.* AUSTIN *enters dressed as Moses.*)

REED: Moses! Moses!

AUSTIN: Oh, God of Abraham! Why do you appear to me in—?

(REED *pretends to accidentally burn his face.*)

REED: Ow!!

AUSTIN: Reed, are you all right?

REED: Austin, am I okay?

AUSTIN: (*Looking at* REED's *head for burns*) Uh, yeah.

REED: Okay. Do the scene.

AUSTIN: Wait a second, I'll be right back—

REED: No, wait, Austin! Let's do the scene—!

(AUSTIN *exits.* REED *looks offstage, out at the audience, shrugs, then starts to juggle the torches.*)

(AUSTIN *enters with a SuperSoaker Fire Extinguisher. He sees* REED *juggling.*)

AUSTIN: That is very impressive.

REED: I know. You can tell by the reaction of the audience.

(*If the audience hasn't started applauding, they will now [except on rare occasions]. Inspired,* AUSTIN *dashes to the keyboard and plays the familiar 3/4 time circus accompaniment.* MATT *enters, sees the circus routine, runs offstage, and re-enters with a pretty tall ladder, which he balances on his chin.*)

(Splashy finish. REED *blows out the torches.)*

REED: Matt, encore!

MATT: No!

REED: Yes! Austin, encore!

AUSTIN: Okay. *(Whispered to* MATT*)* Good luck.

MATT: Thanks.

*(*AUSTIN *does a drum roll on the keyboard.* MATT *lamely dives/steps through a hoop formed by* REED*'s arms. They bow and exit.* AUSTIN *picks up the stone tablets engraved with the Ten Commandments from the wings and walks center.)*

AUSTIN/MOSES: All right, listen up, children of Israel. I've got some good news and some bad news. The good news is, I got Him down to ten. The bad news is, adultery is still one of 'em, so... But there were ten other commandments I talked God out of and right here, in my hand, direct from the home office in Mt Sinai, are the Top Ten Rejected Commandments. Here we go.

(Note: These ten lines are constantly updated to reflect the locale of the performance and topical news stories. This was the list we used recently.)

Number 10: Thou shalt not pee in the swimming pool.

Number 9: Seventies fashions were ugly then and they're ugly now.

Number 8: Thou shalt let the poor fend for themselves. Oh, sorry. No, that's the Republican agenda. *(The audience reacts strongly.)* Gee, I sense some uncertainty out there among you about that one. You know, there's no room for uncertainty in the Old Testament, and I'm the perfect example of that. When I got to the Red Sea I didn't hestitate, I just parted it! *(He gets the SuperSoaker Fire Extinguisher, thus fulfilling the Chekhovian unities, to wit: "If you bring on a SuperSoaker Fire Extinguisher, it must eventually go off.")* Here's one part— *(He squirts one side of the audience.)* —and here's the other part. *(He squirts the other side. And any latecomers. And any random cute girls.)*

Moving right along. Number 7: Thou shalt not tell a lie: *The English Patient* was really overrated.

Number 6: The Christian right is neither Christian nor right.

Number 5: Thou shalt not find parking anywhere in ... *(Insert name of town.)*

Number 4: Thou shalt not waste thy money on ice beer.

Number 3: Thou shalt not blame the entertainment industry for promoting violence or we'll shoot you in the head.

Number 2: Shit happens.

And the Number 1 Rejected Commandment: The English shalt not give back Northern Ireland until the Irish take back "Riverdance"! G'night, everybody!

(AUSTIN exits as MATT enters.)

MATT: And there was great rejoicing and great balls of fire and even more rules and regulations, as set down in Leviticus and Numbers. And in his hundred and twentieth year, Moses did die.

(AUSTIN re-enters with a trumpet on a strap on his back.)

AUSTIN: So God appointed Joshua to become the new leader of Israel.

(REED enters as Joshua, wearing a military helmet.)

REED/JOSHUA: All right, men, ten-hut! We're moving into Canaan at 0600 hours. We're gonna hit the walls of Jericho and hit 'em hard. Our objective: take back the

land which our Lord God and Supreme Commander
has given us. Sound off!

AUSTIN: One!

MATT: Two!

(Pause)

REED/JOSHUA: Okay, that's enough.

(They perform precision choreography.)

REED/JOSHUA: Gather round it's time to go—

AUSTIN/MATT: Gather round it's time to go!

REED/JOSHUA: Kick some ass in Jericho!

AUSTIN/MATT: Kick some ass in Jericho!

REED/JOSHUA: Listen up, now here's the news!

AUSTIN/MATT: Listen up, now here's the news!

REED/JOSHUA: We're taking Israel back for Jews!

AUSTIN/MATT: Taking Israel back for Jews!

REED/JOSHUA: No sound!

AUSTIN/MATT: No sound!

REED/JOSHUA: No noise!

AUSTIN/MATT: No noise!

ALL: Let's go down and kill goys!

REED/JOSHUA: Present horns!

(AUSTIN plays a snappy Latino tune on the trumpet.)

MATT: Joshua, what are you doing?

REED/JOSHUA: This baja marimba salsa always brings
the house down! Left face! Forward run!

(REED *and* MATT *run off and re-enter wearing panchos and shaking maracas.* REED *wears a tiny sombrero and* MATT *wears a Carmen Miranda hat. They march and dance. Big finish.)*

ALL: Oy vey!

REED/JOSHUA: Left-face! Forward march!

(AUSIN *plays* Hava Nagila *as they exit.* REED *addresses the audience.)*

REED: Joshua did indeed bring down the house in Jericho and proceeded to kill audiences all over the Middle East. He slew the people of Midian, known as the Midianites, the people of Girgash, known as the Girgashites, and the people of Paris, known as the French.

(AUSTIN *enters as the Angel of the Lord, complete with wings, halo, green accountant's shade, and a clipboard.)*

AUSTIN: Step right up, ladeez and gentlemen, I'm the Angel of the Lord! Today we're gonna be bargaining with God. I'm gonna auction off God's favors to whoever can suffer the most. So who'll start the bidding off? Who wants to suffer?

(REED *runs on in dark glasses with both arms in slings.)*

REED: I will suffer self-abuse and spill my seed upon the ground.

AUSTIN: Onan, that's not suffering.

REED: Well, it made me go blind. *(He runs off.)*

AUSTIN: True enough. Okay. The bidding stands at spill your seed upon the ground, spill your seed upon the ground...

(MATT *runs on with a stuffed lion.)*

MATT: I'll be thrown into the lion's den.

AUSTIN: Okay, Daniel's going to Detroit!

(MATT *runs off screaming with the lion biting him in the neck.*)

AUSTIN: Detroit, Detroit, Detroit...

(REED *runs on with two baby dolls.*)

REED: The Hebrew children will be thrown into the fiery furnace.

AUSTIN: Okay, now the bidding's heating up.

REED: Hey, we'll need this.

(REED *grabs the SuperSoaker fire extinguisher, shoots the crowd again—particularly any latecomers who were harassed earlier—and takes it off.*)

AUSTIN: *(If there were any latecomers)* Oh, the Old Testament was very tough on latecomers. And the people sitting around them, sadly. Fiery furnace, fiery furnace, fiery furnace...

(MATT *runs on.*)

MATT: My wife will turn into a pillar of salt and die.

AUSTIN: She won't die, Lot!

MATT: Well, she'll die a little. *(Exits)*

AUSTIN: Okay, a pillar of salt, pillar of salt, pillar of salt...

(REED *runs on wearing a rasta wig and carrying a large inflated whale.*)

REED: I'll be swallowed by a whale, mon.

AUSTIN: Okay, Jonah and the Whalers!

(REED *runs off.*)

AUSTIN: All right, the bidding stands at being swallowed by a whale. Come on, this isn't suffering.

Who will show me some *real* suffering? Swallowed by a whale going once, going twice—

(MATT *runs on.*)

MATT: I will buy season tickets for the Los Angeles Clippers. *(Or whatever else is the most boring thing imaginable).*

AUSTIN: SOLD!!!

(MATT *runs off triumphantly.* REED *enters.*)

AUSTIN: Our next item up on the auction block today is slaying the Ammonites. Tell you what—just for laughs, I'm gonna start the bidding off at death to the first person who greets you today.

(REED *laughs.*)

REED: That's good.

AUSTIN: No, I'm serious. It's in the Book of Judges. The first person who greets you today will die in exchange for God slaying the Ammonites. Sound Biblical? Sound completely random? You betcha.

REED: Austin, that's terrible!

AUSTIN: What?

REED: The whole idea that God's favors can be bought and sold.

AUSTIN: Nobody said the Old Testament was pretty.

REED: Yeah, but you make the whole universe sound random and absurd.

AUSTIN: That's life.

REED: No, it isn't. God controls the universe down to the smallest detail. Everything is pre-determined.

AUSTIN: Pre-determined?

REED: Yeah, it's just like professional wrestling!

(Bell rings from offstage. MATT enters as Jacob in a colorful robe. AUSTIN loses his gavel, hat, and clipboard. REED exits to the God mic.)

MATT/JACOB: You're going down, Angel Gabriel!
I don't like the way you make deals with us mortals.

AUSTIN/GABRIEL: Oh, yeah?

MATTJACOB: Yeah!

(REED hits the bell again. Jacob and the Angel begin to fight like professional wrestlers, matching the descriptions below.)

REED: *(On mic)* And there's the bell beginning this unprecedented match between Gabriel and Jacob. Gabriel in the traditional white wings. Jacob has apparently borrowed his son's coat. They seem to be jockeying for position here. It's the cranium crunch, Gabriel is stunned. Ooo, and with that dirty trick, Gabriel proves he's no angel in the ring. Now it's the moral conundrum hold. He throws him up against the cloth. That's gotta' hurt. And now Jacob's got his ladder—

(MATT picks up a small, toy ladder)

REED: *(On mic)* —and with the hit from Jacob's ladder, Gabriel is down and Israel, formerly known as Jacob, is looking for the tag.

(Jacob tags REED who enters wearing a long, blonde wig.)

MATT: *(On mic)* And here comes Samson!

REED/SAMSON: Look what Delilah did to me! *(He pulls off his wig)* She thought she could stop me, but then I joined the Hair Club for Jews. Ha, ha, ha!!

(MATT tags the Angel and wrestles Samson.)

AUSTIN: *(On mic)* And it's Samson versus the Philistine, in a classic matchup. Samson's Seismic Stomp gets the Philistine into the Temple Sleeper Hold, and this one is all over but the mopping up...Oh, my! All that did was piss the big guy off. Ouch! Samson retaliates....

(REED/SAMSON *tosses* MATT *off left, then exits and heaves a full-sized dummy dressed as* MATT *back on stage.* REED/SAMSON *reenters and pummels and throws the dummy around mercilessly.)*

AUSTIN: ...he grabs the Philistine and he throws him out of the ring! This is unprecedented! Now Samson chases him off...and throws him *back* into the ring! Man, oh Manischewitz, Samsom is stomping the stuffing out of this guy. What a dummy! And now he picks him up... and he's biting his ear!!! That's going to cost him in the penalty phase—woah!

(REED/SAMSON *bites the dummy's ear and tosses it upstage through the stage left opening, as* MATT *flies on through the stage right opening. The illusion is that* REED/SAMSON *has thrown the dummy in one door and out the other.* MATT *lies dead on the ground while* REED/SAMSON *raises his arms in triumph.)*

(Blackout. Spot up on REED*)*

REED: I would now like to recite the funniest sections of the Book of Job.

(REED *stares at the audience, then finally shrugs because as we all know, there's nothing the least bit funny in the Book of Job. Blackout. A light rises on* MATT.*)*

MATT: Psalms. The Lord is my Shepherd; I shall not want. He maketh me to lie down in green pastures; He leadeth me beside the still waters. He restoreth my soul; He leadeth me in the paths of righteousness for His names' sake.

(Lights crossfade to REED.*)*

REED: Yea, though I walk through the valley of the shadow of death, I will fear no evil: for thou art with me.

(Lights crossfade to AUSTIN.*)*

AUSTIN: My cup runneth over. Surely goodness and mercy shall follow me all the days of my life; and I will dwell in the house of the Lord forever. Psalms.

(Lights crossfade to REED.*)*

REED: Proverbs. Gossip brings anger as surely as the north wind brings rain.

(Lights crossfade to AUSTIN.*)*

AUSTIN: Better is a dinner of herbs where love is, than a stalled ox and hatred therewith.

*(*AUSTIN *nods knowingly. Lights crossfade to* MATT.*)*

MATT: You better watch out. You better not cry.

(Audience laughs. MATT *doesn't know why.* AUSTIN *and* REED *exit, disgusted.)*

MATT: Shut up! You better not pout, I'm tellin' you why. Proverbs.

(Blackout. Lights up on REED *holding the Ark.)*

REED: Noah's Ark. I know Austin and Matt say we've already done Noah's Ark. I don't believe them, but if it's true, I'm sorry because as I mentioned earlier, it's my favorite Bible story. And not for the reason you might think. It's not 'cause of all the neat animals, but because it's the first time in the Bible that we see a loving and forgiving God, the kind of God that I learned about in Sunday school. And now, as a tribute to the God of Noah and the God I learned about in Sunday school, I'd like to sing my favorite Sunday School song. And I'm sure all of you know this, so please join in with me.

(REED *flicks his cigarette lighter and starts to sing a children's Bible song. Audience joins in.* MATT *joins* REED *onstage and starts singing but then blows out* REED's *lighter in mid-song.*)

MATT: We've done Noah's Ark!

REED: We have not done Noah's Ark!

MATT: We did it Reed, you just spaced out, that's all.

REED: Look, I'm going to prove before the show's over that we have not done Noah's Ark!

MATT: You do that, Reed. I sure hope nothing happens to your little ark.

(MATT *stumbles over the word "nothing" in the previous line.* REED *mock-imitates the stumble when he says "nothing" in the next line.*)

REED: You're right! You do hope nothing happens to my little ark! (*He exits.*)

MATT: (*To audience*) Wise-ass. You don't want to see his little ark. So let's move on. This brings us to the Book of Ruth, which is one of the shortest books in The Bible, making it similar to other short books like *Great Moments of Tolerance in the Old Testament, Positive Images of Women in The Bible* and *Dan Quayle's Guide to Good Spelling (Or something else topical that would make for a very short book)*. And now let's meet an unassuming little shepherd boy by the name of David.

(*Lights up on* REED/DAVID, *who is kneeling in a contraption that has holes for his face and hands, as well as fake feet on the bottom. It makes him look ridiculously small. He holds a tennis racket and ball.*)

REED/DAVID: Fifteen-love. My serve. (*He hits the ball into the wings.*)

MATT/PAL: David, what are you doing?

REED/DAVID: I'm serving in King Saul's court.

(AUSTIN/GOLIATH *enters in some sort of primitive military gear.*)

AUSTIN/GOLIATH: Fee-fie-fo-fum.

REED/DAVID: I see somebody big and dumb.

MATT/PAL: David! Sssshh

REED/DAVID: I'm not scared. The bigger they are, the harder they fall.

MATT/PAL: Discretion is the better part of valor.

AUSTIN/GOLIATH: A rolling stone gathers no moss.

REED/DAVID: Nike. Just do it. *(Or some other popular phrase)*

ALL: Proverbs.

REED/DAVID: Hey, Goliath! Look, it's the land of milk and honey.

AUSTIN/GOLIATH: Really? Are there ponies and cotton candy?

REED/DAVID: Certainly.

AUSTIN/GOLIATH: Cool.

(The lights shift. The actors move in slow motion with slow, melodramatic music; DAVID attempts to poke GOLIATH in the eyes, but Goliath blocks it à la the Three Stooges. DAVID hits GOLIATH in the groin with his racket, doubling him over, then smashes him in the face, sending him reeling. Finally DAVID takes out his slingshot [which is made stiff with wire] and fires a stone at GOLIATH, which MATT carries across the stage in slow motion to hit GOLIATH in the head. GOLIATH falls dead. DAVID and MATT celebrate wildly in slow motion. MATT picks up a sign and shows it to the audience. It says "John 3:16". Blackout. Spot up, down left.)

AUSTIN: David's victory over Goliath is chronicled in the book of Samuel, where we also find the first Biblical reference to motorcycles in the passage, "David's triumph was heard throughout the land".

(AUSTIN *plays a cocktail lounge intro. Lights up on* REED *wearing a crown.*)

REED: Hi, I'm King Solomon and I'd like to sing the new single off my latest album, *Songs of Solomon.*

(REED *breaks into some lame lounge number. After four bars,* MATT *runs in carrying a baby doll.* AUSTIN *resets the keyboard for the next number and exits.*)

MATT: King Solomon, King Solomon, I have a question about yesterday! Are you suggesting that since we can't agree whose baby it is, we should split it in half and let the mothers decide?

REED/SOLOMON: No, I've reconsidered. I personally find splitting babies in half morally repugnant; on the other hand, I'm not sure the government should interfere with a woman's right to choose.

MATT: Good answer. You are wise. I have another question.... (*He chucks the baby into the wings.*) Why does God allow bad things to happen to good people?

REED/SOLOMON: Tough question. Here's another tough question: you know that black box that survives every plane crash?

MATT: Yeah.

REED/SOLOMON: Why don't they just make the whole plane out of that stuff?

(AUSTIN *enters and moves to the head of the line.*)

AUSTIN: King Solomon: the God of the Old Testament is full of anger and vengeance, while the God of the New

Testament is full of love and forgiveness. How can the same God be so different?

REED/SOLOMON: Good question. The answer is "Bewitched".

AUSTIN: You mean "witchcraft?"

REED/SOLOMON: No, I mean *Bewitched*, the T V show. We must simply accept that God can change without explanation, just as we accept that first Dick York was Darren and then suddenly Dick Sargent was Darren. No explanation. Both are Darren—the same, yet different. It's a matter of faith.

AUSTIN/MATT: Ahh!

MATT: What about Elijah the prophet?

REED: Ahh, I believe Agnes Moorhead will portray....

MATT: No, I'm sorry. I'm breaking out of character. I think we skipped something important. What about Elijah the prophet?

REED: Which one?

MATT: Elijah the prophet.

REED: Yeah, which one?

MATT: What do you mean which one? The prophet Elijah. What, are you deaf?

(AUSTIN *runs off.*)

REED: No, Elijah or Elisha?

MATT: I have no idea what you're talking about.

REED: Okay, Elijah with a 'J' or Elisha with an 'S-H'?

MATT: I don't know. How about buttwhiff with 'P-H'?

(AUSTIN *enters with a bunch of hand-held cards with names on them and hands most of them to* REED.)

AUSTIN: Matt! Come on, relax!

MATT: What? I ask a simple question and he makes me feel like a moron.

AUSTIN: Well, go with the feeling. Look, I knew this would be a problem so I brought out the Official Bible (abridged) Flash Cards. These'll spell everything out. Just pay attention. Elijah was the master.

(MATT *holds a large card that says* "Elijah". REED *holds one that says* "Elisha".)

REED: Elisha his disciple.

AUSTIN: Elijah went where God said.

REED: He went there in a trifle. Now Elisha turned prophecy into an art.

AUSTIN: And that is how you tell the two Elishas apart.

(*They have crossed to the keyboard.* AUSTIN *plays. They sing.*)

AUSTIN: Elijah with a "J"
Healed a kid without a suture

REED: Elisha with "S-H"
He could predict the future
If you had lots of lepers
Elisha made 'em better

AUSTIN: If you had phony prophets
Elijah made 'em deader

BOTH: Elijah was the one who went to heaven in a cart
And that is how you tell the two Elishas apart!

MATT: Oh, I get it. What about the two Josephs?
I screwed that up earlier. Is there a way to tell them apart?

(MATT *and* REED *toss their previous cards upstage.* REED
hands MATT *a card that says "Old Joseph".* REED *holds one
that says "New Joseph".)*

AUSTIN: Of course there is. Listen—
Joseph in the old
He had a great life story

REED: Joseph in the new
Accepted his wife's story

(Audiences reacts. The boys do a slow-burn to the audience.)

REED: Well, he did.

*(*AUSTIN *continues.)*

AUSTIN: Old Joseph was a slave
And then he was a leader

REED: New Joseph had a wife
Who became the holy breeder
And had the child who gave Christianity its start

ALL: And that is how you tell the two Josephs apart

AUSTIN: Hosea, Josiah, Isaiah, Jeremiah
Are others in the Bible catalogue
Isaiah had a vision predicting the messiah

ALL: And Jeremiah was a bullfrog!

MATT: This is so helpful. There are so many Johns and
Marys in the Bible. How do you tell them apart?

AUSTIN: Well, it's very complicated so pay attention.

*(*MATT *and* REED *toss the "Joseph" cards upstage.*
REED *hands* MATT *a card that says "John the Baptist"
on the front and "Beheaded" on the back.* REED's *card
says "John Apostle" on the front and "Gospel" on the back.
They reveal the back of the card on the appropriate line.)*

AUSTIN: There was John the Baptist

REED: And there was John Apostle

AUSTIN: One ended up beheaded

REED: The other wrote the gospel

(MATT *and* REED *toss the "John" cards upstage.* REED *hands* MATT *a card that says "Mary" on the front and "Madonna" on the back.* REED's *card says "Mary" on the front and "Tart" on the back. Again, they reveal the back of the card on the appropriate line.*)

AUSTIN: And there were tons of Marys

REED: We don't know where to start

AUSTIN: But listen very closely

REED: And this will make you smart

AUSTIN: The one was the Madonna

REED: The other was a tart

ALL: And that is how you tell the Johns and Marys apart!

ALL: Hosea, Josiah, Isaiah, Jeremiah
Are others in the Bible catalogue
Isaiah had a vision predicting the messiah
And Jeremiah was a bullfrog!

MATT: *Spoken)* What's the difference between ignorance and apathy?

AUSTIN/REED: I don't know and I don't care!

ALL: *(Sung)* Hosea, Josiah, Isaiah, Jeremiah
Are others in the Bible catalogue...

(MATT *makes* AUSTIN *stop playing by pounding on the keyboard.*)

MATT: Wait, wait! After this song is the intermission, right? There's fourteen books in the Old Testament we haven't covered yet.

AUSTIN/REED: No way!

(MATT *points to the contents page in The Bible on the keyboard.*)

AUSTIN: Oh...yah way (*"Yahweh"*). I can do this.
I'll do these fourteen completely, then we can move on. Tick 'em off. Ezekial, Joel, Micah, Obadiah.

ALL: The Book of Lamentations is a hoot.

AUSTIN: Habbakuk and Haggai, Nahum, Zechariah

ALL: Ezra, Malachi, Zephaniah!

(*The music stops.* MATT *turns the page of The Bible, revealing more undone books.*)

AUSTIN: Oh, shoot.
Esther, Amos, and Andy!

REED/MATT: Yes!

MATT: Hey, that reminds me of the ultimate Bible question: What's the difference between Doctor Laura and a bucket of crap?

AUSTIN/REED: The bucket!

ALL: From Creation to Moses to Jonah goin' fishin'
The older of the testaments is through
So now we are going to take an intermission—
And Jeremiah's still a bullfrog!
Hey!

(*Blackout. Intermission*)

END OF ACT ONE

ACT TWO

(Houselights dim to half. The stage is empty, and the audience gradually hears voices over the house speakers. It's MATT and REED talking about whatever's going on that day, or that performance, and "accidentally" being picked up by the God mic. Eventually, as the audience quiets down, they bring the subject around to the weather.)

REED: ...I know, it's freezing in here. It's just like that Bible verse.

MATT: What Bible verse?

REED: You know—"Many are cold, few are frozen."

MATT: That's not a Bible verse!

REED: Yes, it is!

MATT: Where?

REED: New Testament.

MATT: Where in the New Testament?

REED: The Book of Galoshes.

MATT: Really? Hey, Reed, we're going to do the New Testament this act, right?

REED: Yup.

MATT: Well, I wanna tell my parable about Jesus and Moses.

REED: There is no parable about Jesus and Moses.

MATT: Wait a minute—has the Second Act started?

REED: Matt, think about it. If the Second Act had started, we'd be doing something funny now, wouldn't we?

MATT: Not necessarily. Anyway, Jesus and Moses are out golfing one Sunday morning.

REED: Sunday morning?

MATT: Okay, Saturday morning.

REED: So they're golfing on the Jewish sabbath?

MATT: Tuesday morning, nine-fifteen, behind the Johnsons!

REED: Okay.

MATT: They get to the seventeenth hole—par three over water. Moses tells Jesus he better use a seven iron, or else he'll never make it over the water. But Jesus says "Uh-uh, I saw Tiger Woods do this. If he can do it, I can do it". So Jesus hits the ball and it goes into the water. So Jesus asks Moses to part the water so he can get his ball. Moses says, "Okay, but I'm only going to do this once." So Moses parts the water, Jesus runs out, gets his ball, puts it back on the tee and then he asks Moses if he can have a Mulligan. Now...

REED: Wait a minute. What's a Mulligan?

MATT: Oh, I'm sorry. A Mulligan is a religious term for another shot without penalty.

REED: Oh. Like confession.

MATT: Right. So Jesus hits the ball again and again it goes into the water. Jesus asks Moses if he can part the water, and Moses says, "Look, I told you I would only do this once."

REED: Wow, Moses is a real hard-ass.

MATT: Well, he was abandoned as a kid, Reed. You know how that is....

REED: Yeah, that's tough.

MATT: So anyway, Jesus goes walking across the water to get his ball. Just then, the foursome from behind come up. They see Jesus walking on water and go to Moses and say, "Hey, who does that guy think he is, Jesus Christ?" And Moses says, "No, Tiger Woods."

REED: You know what, Matt?

MATT: What?

REED: I'm fairly certain we won't have enough time for that particular parable.

MATT: Oh, come on...

AUSTIN: Hey, you guys haven't touched my God mic, have you?

REED: Don't worry, we haven't touched it.

MATT: Hey, why is it Austin's God mic? How come he's the only one who gets to play God? I should be playing God.

REED: Matt, why should you be playing God?

MATT: Because I play all the women.

(The audience usually cheers, but not always.)

REED: Wait a minute—Matt, you're saying that God is a woman?

AUSTIN: No, Reed, I think he's right. In the Book of Malachi, God actually refers to Herself as "the wife of Israel".

REED: Huh.

AUSTIN: Also, in Genesis 28:16, Jacob says, "Surely *(Shirley)*, the Lord is in this place."

MATT: Hey you guys, I'm pretty sure the Second Act has started. I think they've been sitting in the dark for like five minutes.

REED: Well frankly, judging by their reaction, I think they were in the dark the whole First Act.

AUSTIN: Maybe. You guys ready? We gotta go out there now and be the Wise Men. Pull yourselves together. Try to show a little dignity.

(We Three Kings *plays and the three boys enter, dressed as the Three Wise Men,* AUSTIN *and* REED *with traditional robes and headwear,* MATT *wearing a silly-patterned robe and a Brocabrella on his head. They carry gift bags.* MATT's *carrying a map. They look around, lost.* MATT *puts the map on the floor and points to a spot. The other two gather around.)*

ALL: Ahh! Follow me!

(They each walk in a different direction, then notice that nobody's following.)

MATT: Hey!

AUSTIN: Hey, I thought you were following me!

MATT: I thought you were following me!

REED: I thought we were following the Star.

AUSTIN: The star that shines brightly above a humble stable?

REED: No, The Star! *(He holds up a tabloid newspaper and reads the headline which is visible to the audience)* "Virgin Mary has space alien's baby in Bethlehem."

AUSTIN: No, we're following me. Come on, I'll get us there.

REED: Oh, that's so like an Aries. Always gotta be in charge!

AUSTIN: Typical Sagittarius! Judgmental and angry!

REED: I am not judgmental and I am not angry!

AUSTIN: Ya-huh!

MATT: Wise men! Wise men! Come on Balthazar, come on Louie! We don't believe all that 'what's-your-sign?' hooey, do we, Louie?

AUSTIN: Of course we do. We're astrologers.

REED: Astrological signs dictate every facet of a person's life.

MATT: They do not!

REED: They do too!

MATT: They do not!

REED: Okay, what sign are you?

MATT: Virgo the Virgin.

REED: I rest my case.

(They look at the sky.)

MATT: Of all the nights for the Middle East to be overcast.

AUSTIN: We better hurry, or we won't be there in time for Christmas.

MATT: I want to make sure he gets my present.

AUSTIN: He's gonna love what I got him.

MATT: I don't know, Louie. Mine's pretty valuable.

REED: I got you guys way beat.

AUSTIN: I'll show you mine, you show me yours.

ALL: One, two, three!

(They reach into their gift bags and pull out three identical baseball mitts.)

MATT: I thought you were getting him gold.

AUSTIN: I thought you were getting him frankincense.

MATT: *(To* REED*)* I thought you were getting him myrrh.

REED: What *is* myrrh?

MATT: I think it's a Russian space station. That's why I bought him a baseball mitt.

REED: Doesn't look like it's going to clear up anytime soon.

MATT: Let's play catch.

REED: We can't. We don't have a ball.

*(*MATT *reaches into his bag and pulls out a baseball.)*

MATT: I bought him a ball, too.

AUSTIN/REED: Kiss ass.

*(*AUSTIN *heads down right,* REED *down left,* MATT *up center. They play catch.)*

REED: Y'know, the birth of this Messiah is going to create a whole new set of theological questions.

AUSTIN: Ah, yes, theological questions. You know, "theological" is one of those self-contradicting words, because "theo" means God, and belief in God is based on faith while logic is based on reason. So, "theological" is an oxymoron. Like "Christian Science".

MATT: Yeah, or *(Insert name of local idiot here, like Kato Kaelin or...)* John Rocker.

REED: John Rocker isn't an oxymoron.

MATT: You're right. He's just a moron.

AUSTIN: So under this new theology, what'll be the Seven Deadly Sins?

REED: Same as always: Vanity, Lechery, Wrath, Sloth, Gluttony, Envy, and Avarice.

MATT: Wait a minute. Sloth and gluttony? What about murder or rape?

AUSTIN: No, those are okay. But God help you if you're fat and lazy.

MATT: Do you suppose God has a sense of humor?

AUSTIN: He must. He made people with a sense of humor.

REED: Yeah, and get this. He led the Children of Israel throughout the Middle East for forty years, and had them stop in the one place with no oil.

(They laugh, then all look heaven-ward and give a thumbs-up.)

ALL: Good one!

MATT: Look! A shooting star! Hey, the sky's cleared up. Let's go.

(They put their mitts back in their bags.)

AUSTIN: Wait, I'm confused. What are we supposed to do when we get there?

REED: We worship the Christ child and then we give him his birthday presents.

MATT: Wow—his birthday falls on Christmas? Tough break.

REED: Yeah. And after that we go to the four corners of the earth and spread the good news of love and forgiveness.

AUSTIN: What good news of love and forgiveness?

REED: You know, accept Christ or burn in hell.

MATT: Ready?

AUSTIN/REED: Yep.

ALL: Follow me.

(They each exit in different directions, as music plays again. AUSTIN enters as JOSEPH. REED enters as a SHEPHERD holding a toy sheep.)

REED/SHEPHERD: Oh, Joseph, don't be that way!

AUSTIN/JOSEPH: Oy, I can't believe it. I can't believe Mary is pregnant. We haven't even known each other yet.

REED/SHEPHERD: Well, how did it happen?

AUSTIN/JOSEPH: She said the Angel of the Lord came upon her.

REED/SHEPHERD: The Angel of the Lord came upon her? Well—

AUSTIN/JOSEPH: Leave it alone, leave it alone. That's not what I meant. Besides, that's ridiculous. That's like saying she slept with a ghost. Can you believe that?

REED/SHEPHERD: Sure. I've done it.

AUSTIN/JOSEPH: Really? You've slept with a ghost?

REED/SHEPHERD: Oh, I'm sorry...

(Audience laughs and groans as they understand the implication.)

REED/SHEPHERD: Get the feeling that they're a little ahead of us?

AUSTIN/JOSEPH: Yeah, and I'm a little surprised.

REED/SHEPHERD: *(Back in the scene)* No, I'm sorry. I thought you said goat.

(MATT *enters as* MARY, *with a baby doll high up between his legs under his skirt.*)

AUSTIN/JOSEPH: No, *ghost*, like Casper the Ghost—

MATT/MARY: Joseph, it's time!

AUSTIN/JOSEPH: Oh, my gosh! Quick, go get towels and hot water!

REED/SHEPHERD: Yes, sir! *(Exits)*

AUSTIN/JOSEPH: Try to get comfortable, Mary.
(He helps her to the ground.)

MATT/MARY: Uh-oh, it's coming!

AUSTIN/JOSEPH: Now?! Holy sheet!

REED/SHEPHERD: *(Entering with a sheet)* Yes, sir.
Right here.

(He covers MARY *from the neck down with the sheet.)*

AUSTIN/JOSEPH: Remember to breathe, Mary!

MATT/MARY: Breed?

AUSTIN/JOSEPH: No, not breed. Breathe!

MATT/MARY: Ohh—it's coming! AAAAaaaaa!!!

(MATT slingshots the baby to AUSTIN *[with a hidden bungee cord under his skirt which hooks around each of his sandals] who catches it.* REED *rips off the sheet.)*

AUSTIN/JOSEPH: *(Holding up the Baby)* Jesus H. Christ!

MATT/MARY: Yes! We will name him Jesus!

(AUSTIN hands MATT the baby. All three cross U C and sing.)

ALL: We wish you a merry Christmas!
We wish you a merry Christmas!
We wish you a merry Christmas!
Our dear son of God!

For he's a jolly good savior
For he's a jolly good savior
For he's a jolly good savior—
Who Peter will deny! Aww!

(Blackout. A special comes up on AUSTIN.*)*

AUSTIN: The Christ-child fled into Egypt to escape
Herod's wrath. At age twelve, he amazed the Elders of
the Temple with his knowledge of Scripture. But then
there followed a mysterious eighteen-year gap in the
life of Jesus. At age thirty, Jesus suddenly reappeared
and then went to the River Jordan to be baptized.
Ladies and gentlemen, I give you—the one, the
only—Jesus of Nazareth.

*(*AUSTIN *exits.* REED *and* MATT *enter wearing identical
Jesus outfits: matching beard and robes. They cross
downstage in matching steps and speak in unison.)*

REED/MATT: John the Baptist, I have come from Galilee
to Jordan to be baptized by you. *(They look at each other)*
Hey! What are you doing? *(They point to themselves)*
I'M playing Jesus! *(They point to each other)* No, YOU'RE
playing John the Baptist!

*(*AUSTIN *enters, dressed exactly the same.)*

ALL: Wait a minute, *I'M* supposed to play Jesus!
YOU'RE supposed to play John the Baptist and
YOU'RE supposed to play Mary Magdelene.

AUSTIN: C'mon, let's be fair about this. We should
all get to play Jesus; that way, we can each bring our
own special quality to the role. I can bring scholarly
pomposity; Matt, you can bring childlike innocence;
and Reed, you can bring...

REED: The ark.

AUSTIN: Exactly.

REED/MATT: Yeah, okay, et cetera.

AUSTIN: I'll start off by playing John the Baptist,
but then we're trading off. *(Exits.)*

REED/MATT: Yeah, okay, et cetera. And now, ladies
and gentlemen, John the...*(To each other)* SHUT UP!!

(They throw up their arms and exit. AUSTIN *enters as* JOHN
THE BAPTIST.*)*

AUSTIN/J T B: Step right up, my brethren! Step right up,
my sistern. I'm here to prepare ye for the way of the
Lord! Can I get an amen for the way of the Lord?
(Audience says a lame "Amen".) Now ya'll can do better
than that. *(He pulls a heavy-duty spray bottle out of his
pocket.)* Unless you want me to start baptizing you now!
Now let's try this again. And this time, do not deny
your faith! Denial is not just a river in Egypt! I said—
(Somebody groans) I heard that! *(He squirts the groaner.)*
Everybody's a critic. Now let's try this again. Can I get
an amen for the way of the Lord? *(Bigger response)*
Thank you, Jesus!

*(*REED *enters as* JESUS, *and says his line almost in* AUSTIN's
ear.)*

REED/JESUS: You're very welcome.

AUSTIN/J T B: *(Gasp)* I have preached all along that
there cometh one mightier than I after me, the latchet
of whose shoes I am not worthy to stoop down and
unloose.

REED/JESUS: I'm not sure what you said but I think
you're talking about me.

AUSTIN/J T B: I'm talking about you! Will you be
cleansed by my holy waters?

REED/JESUS: That is why I am here.

AUSTIN/J T B: Be purified and cleansed of all sin!
(He spritzes our Lord in the forehead.) I baptize you in

the name of the Father *(Spritz)*, and...of You *(Spritz)*, and of the Holy Spirit!

(REED holds up his hand so AUSTIN spritzes it instead of REED's forehead for the fourth time.)

REED/JESUS: Don't push it, John. I'm your cousin. You know who I am, don't you?

AUSTIN/J T B: Yes! Your coming was foretold by Elijah the prophet.

REED/JESUS: Which one?

AUSTIN/J T B: The one who—

BOTH: Went to heaven in a cart.

REED/JESUS: Got it.

AUSTIN/J T B: He also foretold that I would appear to preach prior to your arrival, *and* that you are the Messiah!

REED/JESUS: He was correct.

AUSTIN/J T B: And that I would do this.

(AUSTIN spritzes our Lord again. REED struggles to stay calm.)

REED/JESUS: I'm going to turn the other cheek now.

(REED turns away. AUSTIN spritzes his butt. REED turns quickly back to face AUSTIN.)

AUSTIN/J T B: Oh, Messiah, will you now baptize me?

REED/JESUS: Oh, no, John the Baptist. I have something a little better planned for you. Behold!

(REED snaps his fingers and exits. Music. Light change. MATT enters dressed as SALOMÉ, dancing.)

MATT/SALOMÉ: I'm Salomé, that is my name
I am an evil lass

Boys love the way I dance all night
They always grab my mule.

I'm bored with life, of life I'm bored
It's a fact that has been provéd
So I will marry Herod
Who's my uncle twice-removéd

AUSTIN/J T B: Oh no! Oh no! That cannot be!
With your uncle, don't be coital!
I don't believe incest is best
It makes kids mongoloidal!

MATT/SALOMÉ: Take him away! Get him gone
And give a girl some peace
After all, I'm Herod's Queen
And not just Herod's niece

AUSTIN/J T B: Aahh! *(He exits.)*

MATT/SALOMÉ: But now I fear I'm bored again
Life is a boring state.
But what would pique my interest
Is a head upon a plate.

(REED rolls on a table with a large platter on it.)

MATT/SALOMÉ: Oh, look, oh, look, oh lookie there
A platter I do see-eth
Reed Martin, would you lift the lid
And show what's undernee-eth?

*(REED lifts the lid. AUSTIN's head is sticking up through a
hole in the table and platter, his body is hidden underneath.)*

AUSTIN/J T B: It's John the Baptist, it is I
I'm feeling kinda bad
I don't think I shoulda spritzed our Lord
I think I made him—

(REED spritzes AUSTIN.)

AUSTIN/J T B: Hey! Stop it, stop it! Lights! Lights!
Turn out the lights...

(Blackout. Lights up on REED.*)*

REED: As we clearly demonstrated in the previous
scene, John the Baptist did indeed have reason to cry in
the wilderness. And after Jesus was baptized, Our Lord
reached an epiphany.

*(*REED *exits.* MATT *enters as* MARY.*)*

MATT/MARY: Jesus! Jesus! Come in for supper!

*(*AUSTIN *enters, carrying a hunk of wood and a piece of
parchment.)*

AUSTIN/JOSEPH: Mary, Mary! Look what I found in my
carpentry shop!

MATT/MARY: What is it?

AUSTIN/JOSEPH: It's a note from Jesus!

MATT/MARY: Oh, dear. "Dear Mother and F...Joseph..."
I'm sorry, honey...

AUSTIN/JOSEPH: That sucks.

MATT/MARY: He loves you.

AUSTIN/JOSEPH: *(Sulking)* He loves everybody. Read
the note.

*(*MATT *and* AUSTIN *mouth the words of the note as we hear*
REED*'s recorded voice-over.)*

REED: *(V O)* "Dear Mother and Joseph, I just don't feel
I have what it takes to be a good carpenter. So I'm
leaving to wander in the wilderness for forty days and
forty nights to, well, get my head together. Don't worry,
I'll be fine. Love, your miracle, Jesus. P S: Hope you like
the ashtray."

(AUSTIN *and* MATT *look at the hunk of wood with six nails bent in at odd angles.*)

MATT/MARY: But can you earn a living as a Messiah?

AUSTIN/JOSEPH: No, that's why I wanted him to go into his father's business.

MATT/MARY: He is.

AUSTIN/JOSEPH: No, my business! I mean, look at that. It's embarrassing!

MATT/MARY: But if I could just know that he's all right.

AUSTIN/JOSEPH: But, Mary, you must have faith! Jesus can fend for himself. Don't forget, He spent all those years with me. Remember, Jesus is a carpenter.

MATT/MARY: Jesus is bulimic?

AUSTIN/JOSEPH: No, He's a craftsman. He can build things with wood. Remember His first project as a carpenter?

MATT/MARY: "There's a Kind of Hush"?

AUSTIN/JOSEPH: No, the Ashtray of Turin...!

(*By this time,* REED *has entered from the back of the audience carrying his model of Noah's Ark. He gets the audience to chant "Noah, Noah, Noah". They begin to clap in rhythm, as well.* MATT *and* AUSTIN *cease their stream of bad Carpenter jokes and try to get* REED *and/or the audience to stop. Finally,* AUSTIN *whistles loudly to stop the noise, ultimately spitting all over the stage.*)

AUSTIN: The hell are you doing?!

REED: Noah's Ark!

AUSTIN/MATT: We've done Noah's Ark!!

REED: I've been doing a little research. I spoke to many of these fine people at the intermission. I spoke to

(Somebody) from *(Someplace local)*, a biblical scholar.
He says we have not done Noah's Ark. I spoke to
(Somebody else) from *(Someplace else local)*, She says we
haven't done Noah's Ark. And incidentally, there's a
fella' named Bill who wants Matt's phone number.

(MATT and AUSTIN double-take to the audience, looking for Bill.)

REED: Now we should do Noah's Ark!!

AUSTIN: No! We're not going to do Noah's Ark, so just
take it off stage...

MATT: Wait, Austin, wait—I think he's got a point.

AUSTIN: What?!

(MATT crosses to REED.)

MATT: May I?

REED: You'll be careful?

*(MATT just takes the Ark without even acknowledging
REED's concern.)*

MATT: I mean, the whole audience was chanting.
They want to see Noah's Ark.

AUSTIN: I don't believe this. You just do anything Reed
says, don't you?

REED: He does not!

AUSTIN: Yes, he does. He does anything anybody says!

REED: He does not!

AUSTIN: Reed, if I said "Matt, throw down that Ark,"
he would throw—

*(MATT throws the Ark onto the ground and it breaks into
a million pieces. REED falls prostrate on the floor, shattered
as his precious Ark. AUSTIN stands there horrified.
MATT kneels down and gingerly picks up some pieces.)*

MATT: Reed, I can't help but feel somewhat responsible for this.

REED/AUSTIN: Somewhat!?!

(REED *charges the Ark.* MATT *thinks he's being attacked and backs quickly away.* REED *starts to gather up the pieces.*)

MATT: What'd you say that for?

AUSTIN: What'd you DO that for?

MATT: Man, we better do Noah's Ark or he may kill himself.

AUSTIN: Or something serious. What are we gonna do? You broke it into a million pieces.

(*They begin to help* REED *gather up the pieces and scattered animals.*)

MATT: Well, we can make the stage the Ark. It's big enough.

AUSTIN: It doesn't matter how big the stage is. The point of Noah's Ark is the animals, right? Hello? Noah's Ark was loaded with animals and there's only three of us. Where are we going to find hundreds of animals?

(*Beat. All three do a slow look to the audience.*)

MATT: Well, they've been acting like animals all night.

AUSTIN: Matt, let's gather them two by two!

REED: Guys, this is stupid...!

AUSTIN: Reed, if you can clear this stuff away, I think we can do Noah's Ark...

MATT: Could I get some house lights? Uh-oh, it's starting to rain...

(MATT *and* AUSTIN *go into the house and get five pairs of volunteers.* REED *clears the broken ark and then brings on three pairs of animal noses, two fish puppets, and two plastic bananas which he gives to* AUSTIN. REED *also hands* AUSTIN *a clipboard with paper and a pen.* AUSTIN *dresses the five pairs of audience members: two pigs, two ducks, two cod, two cats, two gorillas. With the exception of the ducks, it is preferable for each of the pairs to consist of one male and one female memeber.* AUSTIN *makes them stand shoulder-to-shoulder upstage.* REED *has crossed down to lean against the proscenium, totally unconvinced about the wisdom of this.)*

REED: I can tell this is going to suck.

MATT: Ladies and gentleman—this one's for Reed—Noah's Ark!

*(*MATT *gets the audience to applaud.* AUSTIN *and* MATT *start to sing.)*

AUSTIN/MATT: *(Singing)* Old man Noah had an ark
Ee-aye-ee-aye-oh
(They lead the two pigs downstage.)
And on that ark he had two pigs
Ee-aye-ee-aye-oh
With a...

PIGS: Oink! Oink!

(Inevitably, everything grinds to a halt.)

REED: Oh, yeah, these pigs are really gifted! *(He goes into the house and sits in an empty seat.)*

AUSTIN: *(To the pigs)* Don't worry about him. He's just jealous. Now, your energy was great but we really need a snort. *(He demonstrates a snort)*. Can you try that?

(They snort.)

AUSTIN: Okay, let's try it again! Nice and loud, you know what to do.

AUSTIN/MATT: With a...

PIGS: Snort, snort!

AUSTIN/MATT: Here. And a...

PIGS: Snort, snort!

AUSTIN/MATT: There. Here a...

PIGS: Snort!

AUSTIN/MATT: There a...

PIGS: Snort!!

AUSTIN/MATT: Everywhere a...

PIGS: Snort, snort!

(AUSTIN *and* MATT *get the crowd to applaud, and keep singing. They take the two pigs back upstage. They bring down the next pair of volunteers. It is preferable for this pair to be two women.*)

AUSTIN/MATT: Old man Noah had an ark
Eee-ay-eee-ay-oh!
And on that ark he had two ducks
Eee-ay-eee-ay-oh!
With a...

DUCKS: Quack, quack!

REED: *(From the house)* Wait a minute, wait a minute! You guys have made a huge mistake!

AUSTIN: What?

REED: What good is it going to do Noah to have two female ducks?

AUSTIN/MATT: Ohh...

AUSTIN: Well, I guess Noah was more progressive than we thought. Don't worry, Reed, this is a perfectly good pair of dykes and—DUCKS!!! Ducks!! Oh, I'm really sorry...

MATT: Yeah, we don't care what you guys do in your personal life.

AUSTIN: It's none of our business. That was just a slip of the tongue. So here we go, you know what to do, nice and loud...

AUSTIN/MATT: With a...

DUCKS: Quack, quack!

AUSTIN/MATT: Here. And a...

DUCKS: Quack, quack!

AUSTIN/MATT: There. Here a...

DUCKS: Quack!

AUSTIN/MATT: There a...

DUCKS: Quack!

AUSTIN/MATT: Everywhere a...

DUCKS: Quack, quack!

(MATT *and* AUSTIN *walk them upstage and bring down the fish.)*

AUSTIN/MATT: Old man Noah had an ark
Eee-ay-eee-ay-oh!
And on that ark he had two cod
Eee-ay-eee-ay-oh!
With a...

(The cod are baffled as to what they should do. REED's *had enough.)*

REED: Okay, that's it! That's it! *(He climbs back onstage)* Look, you guys are embarassing yourselves, you're embarassing the audience, you're embarassing all these fine people who volunteered. You've made another huge mistake.

AUSTIN: What?

REED: Think about it: there would be no cod on the Ark.

MATT: Ohh, no sea-creatures on the Ark itself.

AUSTIN: Right, 'cause the saltwater's rising—

REED: They wouldn't be cod on the Ark. Obviously, they'd be trout. So first of all, we need you to swim. *(He imitates the swimming motion and the cod follow suit.)* Very good. Now it turns out trout are the noisiest fish in the water. They make kind of a whale sound—like this. *(He makes a big inhaling sound.)* Can you try that? *(They do.)*

AUSTIN: Great! Now let's put the vocal *(He demonstrates the sound again.)* and the physical together for the total trout.

MATT, AUSTIN & REED: With a...

TROUT: *(Inhale, inhale)*!

MATT, AUSTIN & REED: Here. And a...

TROUT: *(Inhale, inhale)*!

MATT, AUSTIN & REED: There. Here a...

TROUT: *(Inhale)*!

MATT, AUSTIN & REED: There a...

TROUT: *(Inhale)*!

MATT, AUSTIN & REED: Everywhere a...

TROUT: *(Inhale, inhale)*!

(They get the audience to applaud and then lead the trout upstage and bring down the two felines.)

MATT, AUSTIN & REED:
Old man Noah had an ark
Eee-ay-eee-ay-oh!
And on that ark he had two—

MATT	AUSTIN	REED:
Panthers!	Pumas!	Cats!

MATT, AUSTIN & REED: *(They look at each other.)* Eee-ay-eee-ay...oh...

REED: They're cats.

AUSTIN: Pumas.

MATT: Panthers.

REED: Cats.

AUSTIN: I thought they were pumas...maybe lemurs.

REED: Lemurs?!.

(They kneel down. REED draws on the clipboard to show what he's talking about.)

REED: Austin, a lemur is a marsupial and has a pouch.

AUSTIN: No, you're right. I meant pumas.

REED: But the puma has a curvature here.

AUSTIN: Look, my point is they're too big to be ordinary housecats. They're like five, six feet tall.

REED: Well, look at the damn... *(Whatever set of animals is the tallest).*

MATT: No, you guys are missing the point. Look at her *(Indicating the female cat)*. What does she look like to you?

AUSTIN: A fox.

MATT/REED: Stop it! Knock it off!

AUSTIN: She's pretty!

MATT: I know she's pretty, but... *(Drawing)* ...see how her nose kinda tapers? Now, look, if I finish the drawing...they're alligators.

AUSTIN: No... *(Turning the drawing ninety degrees)* ...they're Italy, according to this.

REED: Yeah, they're Italy.

MATT: That's not fair, I can't draw.

REED: But look at those whiskers... *(Drawing again)* ...those are what make them domesticated animals.

MATT/AUSTIN: Oh yeahhhh....

AUSTIN: You're definitely right.

REED: Sorry about that. Sorry.

(They stand up and dust themselves off. They carry on with the song.)

MATT, AUSTIN & REED:
And on that ark he had two ordinary housecats
Eee-ay-eee-ay-oh!
With a...

CATS: Meow, meow!

MATT, AUSTIN & REED: Here. And a...

CATS: Meow, meow!

MATT, AUSTIN & REED: There. Here a...

CATS: Meow!

MATT, AUSTIN & REED: There a...

CATS: Meow!

MATT, AUSTIN & REED: Everywhere a...

CATS: Meow, meow!

MATT, AUSTIN & REED:
Old man Noah had an ark
Eee-ay-eee-ay-oh!

(They get the audience to applaud, then lead the two cats upstage and the two gorillas downstage.)

MATT, AUSTIN & REED:
And on that ark he had two gorillas
Eee-ay-eee-ay-oh!
With a...

(Sometimes they need help with the physical aspect: scratching armpits, beating breasts, eating lice off each other's hair. Usually it's best to just get through it.)

AUSTIN: You can pound on your chests.

REED: Or scratch your armpits.

MATT: You can pick lice out of each other's hair.

(They demonstrate picking lice on each other and the two gorillas.)

AUSTIN: You could throw your own vomit, but I wouldn't recommend it. Any of these things would be acceptable. Here we go. Nice and loud. With a...

GORILLAS: Ooh, ooh!

MATT, AUSTIN & REED: Here. And a...

GORILLAS: Ooh, ooh!

MATT, AUSTIN & REED: There. Here a...

GORILLAS: Ooh!

MATT, AUSTIN & REED: There a...

GORILLAS: Ooh!

MATT, AUSTIN & REED: Everywhere a...

GORILLAS: Ooh, ooh!

(They get the audience to applaud and lead the two gorillas upstage with all the other animals.)

REED: The animals have all been fantastic, but you two have still left out one extremely important thing.

AUSTIN: What?

REED: You forgot all the unrighteous people who *didn't* make it onto the ark. They're not represented.

MATT: Oh right, the sinners.

AUSTIN: Gee, where could we find hundreds of sinners?

(They look to the audience.)

REED: All right, why don't you represent all the unrighteous people who drowned in the flood. And to sort of expedite things here, I'll give you a sound and a gesture. So you're sinners, you're drowning, something simple, something along the lines of— *(He makes an hysterical screaming noise and waves his arms for help as he glubs.)* So shall we practice that once? And I want to see everybody doing it. Here we go—

(They do, usually pretty well.)

AUSTIN: Man, you guys know how to sin in this town. *(He exits.)*

REED: Okay, so this will be the big final verse. We'll sing one time through, all the way through the sinners' verse, then we'll come back to each of you animals one more time for your sound and your gesture, so all of you be ready. Matt, line 'em up. *(He does.)* And then all of us in the theatre will sing the final Eee-ay-eee-ay-oh altogether. Huge applause. Big bow. Boffo finish.

(AUSTIN re-enters.)

AUSTIN: Reed, I thought of a way to make the flood more realistic! *(He pulls a SuperSoaker from behind his back.)*

REED/MATT: Yes!

(AUSTIN slowly pumps the SuperSoaker.)

REED: Okay!

ALL: Old man Noah had an ark
Eee-ay-eee-ay-oh
And off that ark he left the sinners
Eee-ay-eee-ay-oh

(AUSTIN *squirts the audience.*)

ALL: With a— *(Audience screams and drowns)*
And a— *(Audience screams and drowns)*
Here a— *(Audience screams and drowns)*
There a— *(Audience screams and drowns)*
Everywhere a— *(Audience screams and drowns)*

(They go in reverse order down the line of volunteers.
AUSTIN *pushes each couple forward for their bit.)*

ALL: With a —

GORILLAS: Ooh, ooh!

ALL: Here and a—

CATS: Meow, meow!

ALL: There and a—

TROUT: *(Swimming motion plus inhale noise)*

ALL: Here and a—

DUCKS: Quack, quack!

ALL: There and a—

PIGS: Snort, snort!

ALL: Old man Noah had an ark—

MATT: *(To audience)* Everybody!

ALL: Eee-ay-eee-ay-oh!!

REED: Everyone take a bow! Give yourselves a big hand!

(MATT collects the costumes and props. REED and AUSTIN escort the folks offstage.)

REED: One more hand for all the volunteers!

AUSTIN: Look, the gorillas are signing autographs. We finally did Noah's Ark, Reed, are you happy?

REED: I'm ecstatic. It was a miracle!

AUSTIN: Yes, but it wasn't the Bible's only miracle.

REED: No.

MATT: That's right. Jesus also made the blind man lame.

REED: Well, that wasn't one of his better miracles.

(REED *exits in disgust, with* MATT *in pursuit.* AUSTIN *moves to a stage-left special and speaks the next intro slowly so the other two have time to set up on the dark side of the stage.*)

AUSTIN: And now, as we race through the last half of the New Testament, we are proud to present to you the adult life of Jesus! (*He strikes a gong hanging from the keyboard.*) Jesus raises Lazarus from the dead!

(*Lights up on* REED/JESUS *kneeling to pray.* MATT/LAZARUS *is laying on bench. Only his head and feet are visible.*)

REED/JESUS: Oh, Father, lift him up. Raise your servant Lazarus. Lift him up.

(*As* JESUS *prays, Lazarus begins to levitate. This is achieved with the aid of two false legs with feet attached on the ends.* MATT *holds the false legs with his hands, which are covered with the sheet. As* MATT *slowly stands up, he appears to float in the air.* JESUS *says, "Doh!" and slaps his forehead. Blackout*)

(*They exit.* AUSTIN *runs on and strikes gong.*)

AUSTIN: Jesus casts out a demon!

(MATT *enters groaning.*)

AUSTIN/FATHER: Oh, my son, my son! What's the matter, tell me, what's the matter?

(MATT *pulls a long string of colored tissue paper out of his mouth. This rolled tissue paper is called a "Mouth Coil" and is available in magic stores.*)

AUSTIN/FATHER: Aah! Jesus, Jesus, a demon has taken over my son!

REED/JESUS: (*Entering with a box in hand*) I've got just the thing. (*As he places the box on* MATT's *head*) Wait a minute, didn't I cast a demon out of him once before?

AUSTIN/FATHER: Yes, but I didn't pay your bill and he got repossessed.

(REED *turns the handle on the top of the box, making it look as* MATT's *head is spinning. This "Spinning Head Box" can be purchased at magic stores. The head turns slowly five times. As the head spins we hear the sound of a ratchet over the house speakers. He stops spinning the box.*)

REED/JESUS: Well?

MATT/SON: I feel great! Thanks!

(REED *spins the box half a turn so that it appears* MATT's *head is now facing upstage while his body is facing downstage.*)

REED/JESUS: You're welcome!

(*All three wave to audience. Blackout.* AUSTIN *strikes the gong.*)

AUSTIN: Jesus feeds the multitudes with bread and fishes! (*Exits*)

MATT/JESUS: Bread!!

(MATT *runs on as* JESUS *carrying a loaf of bread. He flings the slices over the audience. Then he exits, and the audience groans in anticipation.*)

MATT/JESUS: Fishes!! (*He re-enters with a fish bowl filled with water and "goldfish" carved out of carrots. He picks up a wiggly one and flings it at the audience. Then he picks out another one...and bites into it. Alternatively, he can throw Goldfish crackers at the audience.*) Scared you, didn't I? (*Strikes gong*) Jesus Performs Miracles!

(*First, peppy music, then lights come up, one by one, on...*)

(REED, *who makes a scarf appear then disappear, with the aid of a false thumb tip—available at magic stores.*)

(AUSTIN, *who makes a cane appear from under a silk. These collapsible canes are available at magic stores.*)

(MATT, *who flips through the blank pages of a coloring book and then magically flips the same pages and they are full of color pictures. Again, this trick can be bought at magic stores.*)

(REED *makes loops with his thumbs and forefingers like an "O K" signs. He then puts them behind his head and when he reveals them they are intertwined. He puts them behind his head again and then reveals them again and they are no longer connected.*)

(AUSTIN, *who lifts his foot and then sets it down—gesturing with his hands as he does so. The [stupid] illusion is that he is magically levitating his foot.*)

(MATT, *who holds a red scarf in front of his crotch and taps the back of the scarf with a stick. He then drops the stick, "accidentally" revealing the gimmick. [If you hold the scarf at the corners, you can hold the stick behind the scarf using your thumb.]*)

(*They bow.* REED *strikes the gong.*)

ALL: The Last Supper!

(*Lights up, revealing a do-it-yourself Last Supper kit—the famed Last Supper painting with holes where all the faces belong. Each hole has the name of a different disciple under it [onstage and off]. From stage right to stage left the names read—Mark, Stephen, Andrew, Judas, Peter, John, Thomas, Louis, Pauli, Matthew, Bernard, and Simon.* MATT *and* AUSTIN *stick their faces through two of the holes.*)

REED/JESUS: You're all probably wondering why I've asked you here.

(AUSTIN *and* MATT *dash quickly to all the different face holes to speak for all the disciples.*)

AUSTIN/MATT: *(Various)* Thanks. It's good to be here. No problem. Etc.

AUSTIN/JOHN: Why are we all sitting on the same side of the table, that's what I wanna know...

REED/JESUS: Do you love me, John?

AUSTIN/JOHN: You know I do.

REED/JESUS: Do you love me, Mark?

MATT/SIMON: Yes, Lord.

(MATT'*s face is in the* SIMON *hole.*)

REED/JESUS: Simon, why do you speak for Mark?

MATT: What...? Oh, crap...

(MATT *looks quickly around at the front of the picture, sees his mistake, and dashes to the correct face hole.*)

REED/JESUS: Do you love me, Thomas?

AUSTIN/THOMAS: I doubt it.

REED/JESUS: Now you may find this shocking, but I have it on good authority that one of you will betray me.

(AUSTIN *and* MATT *again race from face to face.*)

AUSTIN/MATT: *(Various)* No! I can't believe it! That's terrible! Etc.

AUSTIN/JUDAS: *(In a Peter Lorre voice)* How did he know?!

(AUSTIN *moves to the "John" hole.*)

AUSTIN/JOHN: Is it me, Lord?

REED/JESUS: No, John, you are my beloved. Come here, sit at my feet.

AUSTIN/JOHN: I will.

(AUSTIN *leaves* MATT *alone behind the painting and sits beside* REED. MATT *is forced to portray all the apostles—running from face to face.*)

MATT/MATTHEW: Is it me, Lord?

REED/JESUS: No, Matthew, not you.

MATT/MARK: Is it me, Lord?

REED/JESUS: Noo...

MATT/JUDAS: *(In the same Peter Lorre voice)* Is it me, Lord?

REED/JESUS: *(Mocking)* Is it me, Lord? Is it me, Lord? What do you think, Judas?

MATT/JUDAS: I think you're overreacting.

REED/JESUS: Now I have many things to tell you before I go. Simon, I will rename you Peter, meaning "The Rock".

(MATT *now has to move very quickly to the face hole of each prophet* REED *mentions.*)

REED/JESUS: St Stephen, I'm sorry to say that you will be the first Christian martyr. St Louis, you will become a city on the Mississippi River. St Andrew, you will go to Scotland and invent golf. St Bernard... *(To audience)* Anyone see this one coming?... St Bernard, you will become a large dog that saves skiers in the Alps. And St Thomas...

(MATT's *been racing from hole to hole. He runs to the far end of the drop—to the wrong hole.*)

MATT: Christ...! (*He runs back to the* THOMAS *hole.*) What?!?

REED/JESUS: Why do you take my name in vain?

(MATT *points at* AUSTIN *through Louis' face hole.*)

MATT/THOMAS: How come he gets to sit through the whole scene?!

REED/JESUS: Thomas, don't put your arm through Louis' face! St Thomas, you will become a resort in the Caribbean. Now, let us break bread together.

(REED *and* MATT *exit.* AUSTIN *reprises the* SALOMÉ *rhythms.*

AUSTIN: Then they prayed, they bowed their heads
Each drank a glass of wine.
St Pauli had twelve beers instead
And he was feeling fine.

St Francis loved all animals
The fattest and the thinnest
St Patrick drove away the snakes
While he was pissed on Guinness
(*He hits the gong.*)

AUSTIN/REED: Jesus is crucified!

(AUSTIN *is a Sadducee and* REED *is a Pharisee.*)

REED: I've gotta get going, so let's get to business. What do the Pharisees think?

AUSTIN: The Pharisees think that something has to be done, and soon. What do the Sadducees think?

REED: We agree. But now we have to convince Pilate.

AUSTIN: Right.

(MATT *enters dressed as an aviator: cap, goggles, and scarf on a wire sticking straight out behind him.*)

MATT: Gentlemen!

REED/AUSTIN: Pilate!

(MATT *subtly plays up to the audience, stretching the laughs before generously allowing the scene to continue.* REED *exits in disgust.*)

AUSTIN: Are you through milking it, Pilate? Pilate, the people have spoken. We demand that Jesus be crucified!

MATT: Oh, all right. I wash my hands of the whole thing. Let it be on your head.

(MATT *glances at the audience, then "flies" off, making airplane noises as he exits. The lights go to the night state.*)

AUSTIN: (*Very, very simply*) And then the soldiers led Jesus away, and forced a crown of thorns onto His head. Then they crucified him, and a great darkness fell over the land. And in the ninth hour, Jesus cried out, "Father, into thy hands I commend my spirit." Then came the most beautiful and significant aspect of the entire New Testament— (*He taps the gong lightly.*) Jesus is resurrected.

(AUSTIN *runs off. A brief argument is barely heard from backstage. We hear* REED *say, "No way". Then* MATT *shoves* REED *on all the way to center stage.* MATT *exits. The lights shift to a spotlight on* REED. REED *wears a pink bunny suit [Including a cottontail and big ears] carrying an Easter basket filled with pink and green grass and colored eggs.* REED *glares at the audience.*)

REED: This is so stupid. The resurrection of Christ is the crux of Christian belief and it's got nothing to do with bunnies and chocolate eggs. We demean Easter when we celebrate it like a pagan fertility ritual. (*Reluctantly*)

Christ ascended into heaven. He will come again in glory to judge the living and the dead. And his kingdom will have no end. That is pretty cool. Happy Easter.

(There is an awkward moment. Not knowing what else to do, REED shrugs and exits. The lights fade. Lights up. AUSTIN runs on holding the Bible.)

AUSTIN: The Resurrection of Jesus brings us now to the Book of Jude, who was the servant of Jesus Christ and could take a sad song and make it better. Now, we have a very special treat for you. As you know, there are so many great musicals based on the Bible, you know, like *Jesus Christ Superstar, Oklahoma!* So in the spirit of those musicals, we'd like to present to you now the final book of the Bible in a little something that we like to call....

(REED runs on.)

REED: Wait! Did you say the final book?

AUSTIN: Yeah. *(To audience)* In a little something that we like...

REED: No, we skipped a whole bunch of stuff.

AUSTIN: Like what?

REED: All The Letters.

AUSTIN: Oh, the Letters!

REED: That's all right. I can cover this quickly. These were instructions to early Christians. Two were written by Peter, four by John, fourteen by Paul, and as far as anyone knows, nothing was written by either George or Ringo.

AUSTIN: What did they say?

REED: Basically three things: Love the Lord thy God, Love thy neighbor as thyself, and it says Women:

you're responsible for the downfall of mankind,
so shut up and obey your husbands. (*He exits.*)

AUSTIN: Okay, thank you. And now, in the spirit of—

(MATT *runs on, holding up a silver ax.*)

MATT: Wait, we also forgot this!

AUSTIN: What's that?

MATT: The Axe of the Apostles!

AUSTIN/MATT: Yes!

(MATT *exits.* AUSTIN *goes upstage and puts on a top hat and tail coat that are tossed out from behind the drop.*)

AUSTIN: And now, in the spirit of those musicals that I just mentioned, we would like to present to you the final book of the Bible in a little something that we like to call REVELATION—

(AUSTIN *catches a cane which is thrown from backstage.*)

AUSTIN: THE MUSICAL!

(MATT *and* REED *reenter. They wear identical top hats and tail coats and carry canes. They dance and sing smoothly.*)

REED: Oh, the saved are surrounded with love
And removed to the heavens above
And the damned are in a bit of a jam

ALL: That's Armageddon!

AUSTIN: Oh, the bad know they've made a mistake
They are cast into a fiery lake
It's a goof, unless they are fireproof

ALL: That's Armageddon!

REED: Yes, Satan's awaitin' his comeback supreme
His reign will mean pain for the nasty and mean
And on their head will be seen
A sign the devil fixes

ALL: A tattoo of three sixes!

MATT: The beast, he's a real Antichrist
He's in charge, but he's not very nice
If you're wise, you won't take his advice

ALL: The world is a hell
That hell is the world of Armageddon.

(They speak over the music.)

REED: Yes, Armageddon—the end of the world. And with the end of the world comes the end of our little trip through the Bible. Hope you had a good time.

AUSTIN: And we want to let you know that our next performance is... *(He says the time and place of the next show.)* So if you enjoyed the show tell both your friends.

REED: Yeah, and if you didn't enjoy the show, tell your vicar!

MATT: *(Plaintively)* Bill, call me!

(REED and AUSTIN look at MATT, then at each other, and shrug.)

REED: Anyway, we would say that the Bible is swell!

AUSTIN: Full of sex!

MATT: Blood and guts!

REED: Hope we all did it well

ALL: Or we may end up in hell
We pray we were hysterical
And not simply heretical

(They do a good ol' fashioned Radio City kick-line.)

ALL: So that's it, the complete word of God
As you guessed, we are all rather odd
Uma Thurman has a beautiful bod

You'd all better go
That's the end of the show

Aaahhhh—men!!

(They climb into a pyramid.)

ALL: *(Exclaiming)* Go to!!

(Blachout. Bows)

END OF PLAY

APPENDIX

In the interest of the historical record, we compiled a list of funny jokes and hysterical punch lines we used but gradually replaced over the years. Sadly, we lost the list. Instead, you can look at these.

Other top-ten rejected Commandments (pages 25-26)

Thou shalt have a single European currency when Hell freezes over.

Thou shalt not commit murder in Los Angeles or you'll have to pay a very heavy fine.

Thou shalt not waste thy money on Zima

Thou shalt not tell a lie: *Titanic* was really overrated.

Thou shalt not tell a lie: *Magnolia* was really overrated.

Thou shalt not commit adultery unless thou art a member of the Royal Family—in which case it's required.

Thou shalt not spend forty million dollars to find out what everybody else already knew.

Thou shalt not name an airport after the President who fired the air traffic controllers.

Thou shalt not schedule the State of the Union address on the same night as the O J verdict.

Thou shalt not use heroin on the Prime Minister's plane.

Thou shalt not show me the money!

What the hell do you expect from an airline called Valujet?

Other auction-winning examples of suffering (page 29)

I will buy season tickets to your local terrible sports team! I will sit through an entire Keanu Reeves film festival!

Other short books (page 34)

The Remains of the British Empire
Al Gore's Guide to Dynamic Public Speaking
The Understated Fashion Sense of Dennis Rodman

Other buckets of crap (page 40)

Rush Limbaugh, the Spice Girls, Kenneth Starr, and any local hated public official have all worked here.

BROADWAY PLAY PUBLISHING INC

LONG ONE ACTS
(WRITTEN WITHOUT AN INTERMISSION)

BAL
(IN PLAYS BY RICHARD NELSON
EARLY PLAYS VOLUME TWO)

BEIRUT
(IN PLAYS BY ALAN BOWNE)

BETWEEN EAST AND WEST

THE BEST OF STRANGERS
(IN FACING FORWARD)

FLOOR ABOVE THE ROOF

FLOOR SHOW: DOÑA SOL AND HER TRAINED DOG
(IN PLAYS BY EDWIN SÁNCHEZ)

HAITI (A DREAM)
(IN FACING FORWARD)

HARM'S WAY

THE HELIOTROPE BOUQUET BY SCOTT JOPLIN & LOUIS CHAUVIN

HOLY DAYS

HOUSE OF SHADOWS
(IN PLAYS BY STEVE CARTER)

ICARUS

BROADWAY PLAY PUBLISHING INC

LONG ONE ACTS (CONT'D)
(WRITTEN WITHOUT AN INTERMISSION)

BROADWAY PLAY PUBLISHING INC

PLAYS WITH MORE WOMEN THAN MEN

BESIDE HERSELF

A BRIGHT ROOM CALLED DAY
(IN PLAYS BY TONY KUSHNER)

CHURCH OF THE HOLY GHOST

DAME LORRAINE
(IN PLAYS BY STEVE CARTER)

A DARING BRIDE
(IN PLAYS BY ALLAN HAVIS, VOLUME TWO)

GOONA GOONA

THE LADIES OF FISHER COVE
(IN PLAYS BY ALLAN HAVIS, VOLUME TWO)

MINK SONATA
(IN PLAYS BY ALLAN HAVIS)

ONLY IN AMERICA
(IN PLAYS BY AISHAH RAHMAN)

BROADWAY PLAY PUBLISHING INC

PLAYS WITH MORE WOMEN THAN MEN
(CONT'D)

ON THE VERGE

PECONG

PHANTASIE

RAIN. SOME FISH. NO ELEPHANTS.

SHOW AND TELL
(IN PLAYS BY ANTHONY CLARVOE)

STARSTRUCK

STONEWALL JACKSON'S HOUSE

UNFINISHED WOMEN CRY IN A NO MAN'S LAND WHILE A BIRD DIES IN A GILDED CAGE
(IN PLAYS BY AISHAH RAHMAN)

WHAT A MAN WEIGHS

BROADWAY PLAY PUBLISHING INC

TOP TEN BEST SELLING
FULL-LENGTH PLAYS AND
FULL-LENGTH PLAY COLLECTIONS

ON THE VERGE

PRELUDE TO A KISS

TO GILLIAN ON HER 37TH BIRTHDAY

TALES OF THE LOST FORMICANS

PLAYS BY TONY KUSHNER
(CONTAINING A BRIGHT ROOM CALLED DAY,
THE ILLUSION, & SLAVS!)

THE IMMIGRANT

NATIVE SPEECH

BATTERY

ONE FLEA SPARE

THE PROMISE